Be the Change
FIGHTING CORRUPTION

Kiran Bedi

STERLING PAPERBACKS
An imprint of
Sterling Publishers (P) Ltd.
A-59, Okhla Industrial Area, Phase-II,
New Delhi-110020.
Tel: 26387070, 26386209; Fax: 91-11-26383788
E-mail: mail@sterlingpublishers.com
www.sterlingpublishers.com

Be the Change
Fighting Corruption
© 2012, Kiran Bedi
ISBN 978 81 207 7716 3

All rights are reserved.
No part of this publication may be reproduced, stored in a retrieval system or transmitted, in any form or by any means, mechanical, photocopying, recording or otherwise, without prior written permission of the original publisher.

Cover design courtesy
Achal Paul
BUZZ Communications

Printed in India
Printed and Published by Sterling Publishers Pvt. Ltd.,
New Delhi-110 020.

Dedication

Dedicated as gratitude to ALL those who showed the courage and determination to stand up against corruption, in their own way, alone or collectively, which helped expose the epidemic of corruption in India.

Why this book?

When I started to work as Inspector General Tihar Prisons, in 1993, I was informed that prisoners' rations were being pilfered. The food they got was not only insect infested but also short in entitled quantity. Meaning thereby it was a case of heartless-crass-criminal-corruption being committed by insiders and outsiders.

In my 35 years of police service I saw several situations which had the stench of corruption and dishonesty from persons who were responsible leaders in their own right and supposed to be upholding the law and deliver justice but were doing quite the opposite.

They indulged in favouritism of all sorts for their own professional gains and creature comforts. And also not getting visible.

I used to expose such happenings in appropriate forums based on credible evidence while in the police service. Which is why I was kept away on several occasions, both by some politicians in power and some of my seniors from the epicenter of policing---The Police Headquarters.

Once when a new Police Commissioner took over, and I was senior enough to be positioned in the police headquarters, on our very first meeting he told me,

"You will not write, (as I was regular columnist in certain dailies) nor attend any seminars on police reforms".

I asked, "why Sir"?

He said,

"Because this is what I want".

He wanted me to be enslaved for being a part of his team. I did not comply with his instruction. When he saw me not falling in line, he started to harass me in his own ways.

I was nearing an adverse report which would have denied me my promotion. But I was saved by an invisible hand, called God. The HOW of it is history, documented in another book called, I Dare.

This was corrosive corruption so closely encountered.

What we are seeing all around us today is nothing but loot. Loot of very high scale to the extent we can't count the number of zeros.

And as this started to unfold with the Commonwealth Games exposure, it got my goat. I started to be a part of a collective voice which became louder by the day. At times very shrill, not by choice, but by compelling circumstances. But all for one common cause---a well governed India--- a better India which makes us all prosperous and our next generation secure.

This is the spirit behind this collection in, "You Be the Change!

Views were expressed as per the feelings of the situation as felt and perceived. For me it made me feel lighter writing it.

Hope it gets you involved in the fight against corruption reading this.

If the corrupt can unite as a strong vested interest, why can't we the victims not unite for our own selves?

Be the change! In ways you think you need to! Responsibility is OURS.

Contents

Why this book? v

1. A Wish Speech — 1
2. Dividend of a Dark Past Haunts the Country — 5
3. Civil Servants and Accountability — 8
4. Aam Aadmi's Common Fight — 15
5. Check the Cancer of Corruption — 19
6. Corruption in Police: Five Strong Measures to Stop it — 23
7. Courage is the Need of the Hour — 27
8. Tale of Two Bills: Draft and Graft — 31
9. Anna Fasts so We May Breathe Easy — 35
10. Elections don't Solve all the Problems — 39
11. Electorates as Game Changers — 43
12. After Results, Remind the MLA of Promises — 47
13. Hear Yourself, Then will the Neta — 50
14. It is a Trust Deficit — 54
15. Government was Warned, but it Failed — 58
16. How should the Corrupt be Punished? — 62
17. How to Stop the Fence from Eating the Grass — 64
18. Yes, Saying No is Still a Choice — 68

19.	No Escape to the Corrupt	71
20.	Spread the Movement Against Corruption in your own Way	75
21.	The Enemy Within	79
22.	Three Orbits	82
23.	Wages of Fighting for a Cause	86
24.	Why are We the Land of Scams	90
25.	Will We See a Change in our Lifetime?	94
26.	Live in Resolution, Not Conflict	97
27.	Watch Out for Breach of Trust	101
28.	A Template for Leadership	105
29.	Visionary Leaders	109
30.	Women Against Corruption	113
31.	Traders must get Cracking against Corruption	117
32.	Time for a Million to March Here Too	121
33.	Second Freedom Struggle is On	125
34.	Lambs No More, Silent No More	129
35.	The Way Ahead	133

1
A Wish Speech

What kind of speeches are we hoping and *wanting* to hear from our political leaders and what are we getting? Do our leaders speak on areas of good governance or give foreign policy statements and warnings to our neighbour? Do the issues of *roti, kapada* and *makan* figure as burning ones? How important to the audience are the mandir, the masjid, party leader "A" or party leader "B"?

Interestingly, from what was seen in the recently concluded political rallies, whenever people clapped or cheered, it was over the entertainment being provided by the popular film stars "swinging" or "singing". In some places, individuals with long criminal records were addressing rallies. What did they have to say and with what credibility?

No wonder, in this country, incumbency is becoming a factor which works against the government in power. Another way of describing incumbency is "governance" and "performance". So when there is an anti-incumbency vote, it is also a rejection of the performance of the administration, which is mainly the bureaucracy, as a whole. People require a good administration, one that is efficient, delivers services, solves civic problems, and provides internal security with a vision for the future.

Below is an attempt at a "Wish Speech" which people would have loved to hear and seen translated into action.

This speech is for a victorious leader.

My fellow citizens,

I am grateful to all of you for having chosen me to represent you (in the Assembly or the Parliament). I assure you that I will prove worthy of your trust. I stand before you as a full representative of the entire constituency and not only of those who voted for me. I now represent the interests of all of you, equally.

The problems and issues of the constituency are my priorities. We will identify the essential needs at various levels and work on them. Thereafter, we will collectively declare area-wise priorities and proceed to match them with the available resources. I will publicly declare how I will use my constituency funds, so that all of you can be sure they are being properly utilised.

We will all work collectively to ensure that the money spent is well invested and gives us the maximum benefits possible. We will create local groups of overseers to ensure transparency and people's participation in all projects. We will evolve a system of partnership in administration at all levels of governance, rural and urban.

My friends, we will make our plans and implement them in such a way that in our constituency no child goes without schooling, no adolescent without vocational training, no tube well or industry without power. We will see to it that no one feels insecure and no crime goes undetected. We will organise ourselves so that crimes are prevented. We will work on crime correction and also rehabilitation of wrong-doers. Collectively, we will ensure water harvesting and water management so that we give to our next generation more than what we received.

Together, we will ensure higher productivity in all establishments in our constituency, so that we earn more, employ more, and contribute more to the national exchequer. We will work towards enhancing the quality of life so that our people live in harmony and prosperity.

So you see, we have a lot of work to do. I am confident that we will succeed. I can assure you that whatever actions I expect from you, I shall perform them first.

I will visit different areas so that I am with you, except for the days when the (Assembly or the Parliament) is in session. I will declare my visit programme in advance so that you know when I will be with you for interaction. When I come, I will do so with the district administration, that is, the area Superintendent of Police or the DSP or the SHO, the Deputy Commissioners or SDMs or SDO, and other officials of important agencies so that we can collectively see what is wrong and what is right and what needs to be attended on priority.

> *People require a good administration, one that is efficient, delivers services, solves civic problems, and provides internal security with a vision for the future.*

While I will give you what I must, you too should do your duties and perform your role as a responsible and participative citizen. You have elected me for a limited period and we have lots to do. I do not know whether I will stand for another term, but if I do, it will only be if we can achieve what we have set out now.

Before I close, I publicly declare the assets I or my immediate family owns. And before laying down my responsibility as your elected representative, I will come to declare these again, for you to see what I am leaving with. Come, let us do what we must for the sake of our country and our future generations.

When I wrote this "Wish Speech", I came across two speeches which appear as a silver lining in the current scenario. I felt encouraged that there is a beginning, at least, in this direction.

The first speech was by the new Chief Minister of Punjab, Capt. Amrinder Singh, who said, "This government and administration would be completely transparent and the press would be permitted full access to whatever information they want about the working of the administration."

The second speech was by the Chief Minister of Madhya Pradesh, Digvijay Singh. He said, "India has suffered from excessive governance, which is why the state has to withdraw from many of its traditional roles. I believe administration has to be brought to the door of people."

If these words get translated into deeds, there will not be any anti-incumbency votes, but an avalanche of consensus to carry on the good work.

2
Dividend of a Dark Past Haunts the Country

The violence and the corruption we are suffering today is the result of what we have been sowing since independence. The governance of this country has declined over past several years due to increasing stranglehold of corruption and corrupt practices.

Systematically, vital institutions have been eroded by all the classes in charge—political, bureaucratic, police, corporate, and even the services. The only thing that matters now is acquisition for self and family. The country comes last. And in many cases people have gone overseas as they did not see any future here. This is the truth, whether you can digest it or not.

Instead of strengthening the moral fibre of our country, after a hard-fought battle for independence in which countless Indians sacrificed their present for our future, we compromised at every step for personal gains. The situation has been brought to such a pass that it is becoming hard to find even a single individual in public life whom "We, the People" can truly trust. And even if we find one, we revel in bringing him down—recall Manish Tiwari's apology to Anna Hazare for calling him corrupt "from head to toe".

Who all could have brought this decline—parents, teachers, religious and spiritual gurus, political leaders, or the media? Who has been impacting us the most?

In my personal view it has been the political leadership. This class, barring a few honourable exceptions, has been the cause for the decline. As they became greedier by the day, they hung on to power by hook or by crook, without ever thinking of the long term consequences for the country and the society.

Look at the way they have used the police since independence. They have not allowed it to stand on its own feet. They keep using it for their political agendas. They do not let the leadership develop. Anyone with any element of independent thinking is sidelined. I have personally suffered from this a number of times. Can the civil society do anything about it? Look at the number of times officers are transferred. They are literally brought to their knees for transfers, promotions, postings, or to save the schooling of their children or jobs of their spouses.

The million-plus constabulary has been left to fend for itself. They barely recognise their leader. The seniors rarely reach out to them. The juniors are not heard. They have been left to the mercy of local goons or those who claim proximity to power centres.

Is this the way to run a police department where the majority have to fend for their housing, school for their children, and "additional income" to run their two homes—one in their native place and one in their place of posting? They are rarely allowed leave, as they have to be present in every *bandobast* for the security of the VIPs and their public meetings, which are full of hypocrisy and unfulfilled assurances, taking advantage of simple, ignorant people.

No more. People have revolted now. They have come out openly on the streets to speak against false governance. They have found their voice in banding together. They have seen the strength in non-violence once again, thanks to Anna Hazare.

This country must go back to merit and integrity. The leaders must encourage free speech and open discussion. They must listen to people. They must make their governance inclusive. They must allow growth of leadership. They must set the police free and increase its accountability. They must make the bureaucrats perform or perish.

> *People's faith has to be revived in governance. This requires integrity and honesty.*

The leaders must allow the bureaucrats to give advice freely and frankly and take policy decisions, for which they should take responsibility. The officers must be encouraged to do what they think is right, but the ministers can have the right to overrule. But then the ministers must do so at their own risk. They must not force the bureaucrat to recommend what they, the ministers, want. And the bureaucrats should have the courage to say "No".

People's faith has to be revived in governance. This requires integrity and honesty. Full support to the anti-corruption bill which is before the Parliament now will show the determination and resolve. Once the Lokpal starts working, many more scandals will come up and embarrass the politicians and bureaucrats.

The past cannot be re-written, it has to be endured. But lessons can be drawn—you cannot change the law of nature. You reap what you sow. This country has sown violence, corruption, divisiveness, and hypocrisy. It is reaping the results now.

From the day we start sowing honesty, we will start reaping trust.

3
Civil Servants and Accountability

I would not have survived 35 years in the Indian Police Service if Delhi police had not got the police commissioner system in 1977. The reason is that I had experienced a wasteful, intrusive, and very "amateurish" oversight by some greenhorns belonging to the Indian Administrative Service or the direct recruits from the State Civil Service, who were in their first posting in the field. This was in the areas of law and order, crime control, issuance of certain regulations, and keeping control of administrative policy-making decisions, plus the budgetary controls. To my mind, it was an intrusive overlap, and nowhere a constructive or supportive oversight.

I recall many a demonstration as in-charge of New Delhi area where demonstrations were held by the score every day. We, as the district police chiefs, had to wait for the young (green horn) SDMs to arrive and oblige us by signing a "prior" approval to disperse the crowds. Of course, we had to have an understanding that we will not wait if the situation so demanded. But the truth is that many a times they had to be called merely to fulfil this stipulated formality. And every time they did so, it appeared they were doing the police department a favour. This was simply because, if they did not sign, our actions could be construed as a violation of the law under the Police Act of 1861.

So much for our policing—in 2009 we were still governed by an Act of 1861! While one can blame the legislature for this gross negligence, the bigger problem is still of the *babudom* from the civil services which failed to pursue and get suitable laws passed by the legislators. The fact that Indian policing is still administered by the Act of 1861 is clearly more a failure of the bureaucracy than that of the legislators.

For me personally, the dual control at many levels of crime control and law-and-order management was pretty stifling. I felt that professional officers were not being trusted—even after having been trained extensively and prepared professionally during the formative years at professional academies. We ought to have been made more and more accountable instead, and not have these minimally trained "endorsers" (on police issues), who had to be kept in good humour so that they let us do our unending duties. This is the state of affairs in every police district today and more so where there is no police commissioner system.

Who is blocking the change? The same "endorsers", who else? Today the country has only a handful of cities having the commissioner system. Denial of this system has deprived police officers, stopped their accountability from growing, and kept them dependent on the bureaucracy. The tragedy is that the police services have been systematically kept away from courageous, independent, and self-confident leaders who would have kept the "endorsers" and "controllers" in their place and let the leaders focus on their primary responsibility—development.

The police commissioner system gave young officers of my kind more accountability and responsibility. There was enabling power and responsibility to deal with unlawful assembly without waiting for formal endorsements. And many more powers—there was no excuse any more for blame games.

The police commissioner system was most effective in crime prevention. Things which could only have been done by the endorsers or controllers were worked on under this system with a sense of urgency and commitment. Some examples are: processes of externment of bad characters from their places of operation, peace proceedings in conflicts between two groups, land attachments in cases of apprehended breach of peace due to land dispute, enforcement of traffic regulations or other law-and-order regulations such as tenant verifications, and carrying of arms and ammunition.

All this and much more is in the hands of home departments run by the IAS in those police districts which do not have a police commissioner system. Where is the need for this power to be with the civil services? If it can be given to the police in Delhi, Pune, Mumbai, Ahmedabad, Gurgaon, and a few others, why not Lucknow, Patna, Guwahati, Jaipur, Bhopal, Amritsar, and all other cities with a population as recommended by various commissions (all gathering dust in the offices of home departments run by the bureaucracy)?

It is because the IAS officers at the helm have neither endorsed the transition nor allowed the system to let go their control over the police.

So when the police fail, who goes? Has anyone ever seen or heard the departure of the Home Secretaries? Who are they? Does a common man get to see them?

Civil Servants and Accountability

It is said that civil servants wear thick skins.

As one officer shared in our internal group dialogue,

> ... *civil servants have been given the same job in the Indian political and administrative sphere. Like the Europeans' white man's burden, they too have the responsibility of looking to it that everyone does his job sincerely. This takes up so much of their time and energy that they have no time left for their own work. This is easily seen in any meetings of a district magistrate where he has so much to lecture and so much to guide everyone that nothing is finally left for him to do. That is what you call, "the best of both worlds".*

> *The civil servants rule the roost. In terms of promotions and status they are ahead of everyone else by miles. They are central in the Pay Commission and the Cabinet Secretary is involved in every major decision making process. Yet, when things go wrong, they wash their hands off so clean that one wonders how!*

Here is some more from yet another group dialogue. Identities have not been revealed.

> *Last week Maj. Gen.– called on me. He was an esteemed instructor during our degree course days, and many of the officers would remember him as one of our finest. Indeed, he spent most of his time with the –. He was at*

the war front during the 1962 debacle. He has analysed the event very systematically and his study reveals the following:

- *Pandit Nehru, considered the architect of modern India, suffered a severe stroke of depression from which he never quite recovered. He died in May 1964 at the comparatively young age of 73.*
- *V. K. Krishna Menon was removed from the post of Defence Minister for his incorrect assessment of the situation.*
- *Gen. Thapar, the COAS was sacked. The careers of Lt. Gen. Kaul and scores of other military officers took a "U" turn.*
- *A few thousand soldiers died, many more were wounded, and some were taken prisoners.*
- *The psyche of the country received a severe blow. The loss was considered a national shame.*

The question he asked me was,

Who was the Defence Secretary at that time? And what was the punishment meted out to him?

I have asked several friends and also surfed the internet, but I am unable to find the answer. In all probability, nothing was done to him because he had no role in this!

Maj. Gen.– then took this discussion a step further. He observed that during the recent attack on Mumbai, dozens of soldiers and policemen were killed. The whole nation was shaken. Shivraj Patil, the Home Minister, has lost his prestigious job. The Chief Minister of Maharashtra has been axed and several heads in the government are likely to roll.

Can someone tell us as to what action has been taken against the former or the current Union and the State Home Secretaries or the Chief Secretary of Maharashtra? (– tells me that they will all be "promoted" or re-employed soon, as is the practice, though he does not know why). Having spent many years in and around the South Block, I marvel at the way our government has been structured. The civil servants rule the roost. In terms of promotions and status they are ahead of everyone else by miles. They are central in the Pay Commission and the Cabinet Secretary is involved in every major decision making process. Yet, when things go wrong, they wash their hands off so clean that one wonders how!

A slightly closer examination reveals the secret. I have figured it out this way:

- *They never do anything themselves. They always find someone else to be the head and they know how to reduce him to a "figure head". (In the Pay Commissions, they have a retired judge). However, they place themselves in a position which has the maximum opportunity to influence matters.*
- *After the event, they never face the press or the media. Their role is amorphous.*
- *The seniors amongst them rarely sign a letter or order. Our pension letter is signed by a Director, who is not a directly recruited IAS officer. Only rarely do you find a paper signed by a Joint Secretary. Officers above that level do not sign any document.*
- *They have a strong association. It protects the interests of its members dutifully and diligently.*

So we have our Defence Headquarters in which the postings, promotions, rewards, and punishments of all senior officers are controlled by the civil servants; and they also have the final say in the process of procurement of weapons and equipment, but they are not "responsible" if things go wrong! It is authority without responsibility. For those who may not know, a lowly officer in the Ministry of Defence can have a Deputy Chief of Services posted out, but a Service Chief cannot get even a Desk Officer moved!

When Maj. Gen.– left, I found myself perplexed. What sort of system have we evolved? And how has it survived all these years? It is a bit like a unit in which the clerks are running the unit and the Commanding Officer is so dependent on the Head Clerk that he cannot move without his help!

Can someone give cogent answers to the questions raised by the General?

PS (given by another one of our team members):

Politicians wear the dress of the people they represent, to identify themselves with the masses. Soldiers and policemen wear uniforms. Can someone tell us what the civil servants wear? The answer came from the wag who said,

"Civil servants (barring exceptions) wear thick skins."

The million dollar question is, who will set right this thickness?

No one else but honest and clear headed professional politicians . . .

Who are rare but can be there . . .

4
Aam Aadmi's Common Fight

With increasing mal-governance and decreasing trust in the administration, can we do anything to retrieve this dismal state of affairs? Can we, as citizens, take any specific measures to restore public confidence? And if so, where do we begin? Who takes the lead? Does all initiative begin only from the top?

Ever since civil society groups initiated anti-corruption rallies nation wide, one question which keeps coming back is, what about the day-to-day corruption that people face? The daily harassment is from the kind of corruption which robs a common man of his essentials such as rations, driving licence, response from the police, etc. The harassment is also caused by the demands from the inspectors from departments like municipal, factory, labour, health, food, or safety.

When we talk of "government", does a common man relate it with only the top public officials or those in ranks below too? If the answer is the entire rank-and-file, then blaming the leadership alone is a case of juniors deliberately avoiding their own share of the responsibility.

This further implies that officials do not have to wait for instructions from above to do their own duty, but to do it as their inherent responsibility, without fear or favour. It also means personal responsibility at each level, whether at high-end or line function.

This is what needs to be understood. Everyone in government service is duty bound to serve and fulfil the roles and responsibilities assigned to that position or post. Hence, when we say we do not trust the government or a particular department, we are passing a vote of no-trust against the system as a whole, comprising the rank-and-file, from top to bottom.

So what is the answer to the *aam aadmi's* complaints of harassment at the hands of *aam sarkari* officials who are also *aam aadmi* in other roles? Why is the complaining *aam sarkari* official depriving the poor *aam aadmi* of his basic needs and rights? Why is the small fish eating another small fish? What is compelling them? And are they slaves that they have no choice but to carry out dishonest orders, as some claim? Are their promotions and jobs linked to the amount of money they can extort out of the common man? And most of all, why is the common man giving in?

The need of the hour is of the coming together of the *aam aadmi* to confront the *aam sarkari* official over corruption, by the formation of *aam aadmi seva* centres. These groups of volunteers, comprising women, youth, or neighbours, could blow the whistle against the corrupt. Even five is a handful of strength and becomes a fist when united.

While we must tackle corruption at the top, we must fight it at the bottom too, where it impacts the common man the most. The time has come to raise our voice against corruption at any place and of any magnitude, whether by a lower rank official or the highest ranked one.

Therefore, the coming together of the right kind of like-minded people is needed. People have to form homogenous groups and the "beggar" bribe seekers have to be scared of even asking. We cannot wait for the enforcement machinery to change first. We, the citizens, have to challenge it by our own moral might, a might of unity and homogeneity.

> *The need of the hour is of coming together of the aam aadmi to confront the aam sarkari official against corruption.*

The present generation has been contaminated by the scourge of corruption. We have to save our next generation from being infected or else the country will get eaten up by these "termites and vultures".

We, as people, have to unite non-politically. We have to rise above our personal differences and stop being victims of corrupt officials, whether senior or junior. We have to ring the bell and sound the alarm. We have to put the fear of social shame on corrupt officials.

The country needs to know why we need a tougher law at the centre, called the Lokpal bill. It is because currently there is no one to catch the ones at the top. This is why crores of rupees are lost. Once an effective law is in place, huge sums will be saved and can be used for the development of the nation.

Social groups, acting as citizen service centres or *aam aadmi seva* centres, could become interveners and responders to the bugle against the demand by the "beggars". Due to the absence of public retaliation, these corrupt officials have neither the fear of getting caught, nor the fear of a deterrent punishment. We have to raise the risk of the "beggars" in government service getting exposed, irrespective of the rank. Any one who demands a bribe while "in service for a service" is worse than a "beggar" and must be labelled as one, and given the appropriate punishment!

5
Check the Cancer of Corruption

The recent series of scams is nothing but banditry at the national level and amounts to over two lakh crores! A huge national shame!

The sources of this banditry are the 2G spectrum scam, the Commonwealth Games scam, the Adarsh Housing scam in Mumbai, and the land scams in Karnataka.

The loot in the 2G spectrum scam is nearly double the amount required to provide food security to all Indians, or provide education for all for the next five years as estimated by NIEPA, or eight times the ₹ 22,300 crore health budget for this year.

Tackling corruption in India is like fighting another War of Independence. The problem is that serious. It needs a "selfless" Mahatma Gandhi, supported by a band of passionate crusaders. The revolution needs all—writers, speakers, reformers, role models of substance, and people of respectable means. Most of all, it needs the media to keep up the pressure.

This is because the cancer of corruption has seeped into the very vitals of our governance. Our erstwhile holy cows, namely the armed forces and some members of judiciary, are the latest scalps. Our bureaucracy's babus are the weakest at the top and insensitive at the bottom.

Our private sector is flush with money to entice lesser mortals. Our election systems are breeders of corruption from the very start. Their funding pattern is an initiator of all that ails our system. It starts with obligations which the receiver is indebted to repay. Our opaque system of property purchases, land deals, and acquisitions feeds the parallel economy.

Our vigilance systems are inherently and intentionally kept flawed. They are a weak web where you only go round in circles. No vigilance or anti-corruption wing is independent or is the final authority. Either an agency is recommendatory or it is vulnerable to political influences.

There is also a clear class divide. We have police stations for the poor and the CBI, CVC, and CAG for the rich. There are bails, paroles, and even anticipatory bails through a battery of excessively paid legal support for the rich. There are sweaty, smelly and congested barracks for the poor, while there are air-conditioned hospitals for the well off—all for a sum, depending on the paying capacity.

Clearly, in our country there are two sets of justice, barring miniscule exceptions.

Corruption is the rule, being honest is being naïve. This is the current mindset. Bigger the corruption, more is the surety of walking away with the amassed wealth. Smaller the crime, more are the chances of being caught, suspended, and arrested. Bigger corruption is a sure route to increased wealth and even a governance position.

People know who the corrupt are and why corruption is rampant. Yet we re-elect them time and again. By doing so we accord them legitimacy to amass more money and political power. The country and its "services" and its "servants", barring a few, are on sale. Most of the persons in position of some responsibility seem to have a price—

from the lowest rank to the very top, dependent on dare devilry and nuisance value.

The country needs a total overhaul of its vigilance system. It needs a statutory, independent investigating and prosecuting agency, paid from the Consolidated Fund of India, with its own budget, selected on merit through talent search, with fixed tenure to ward off political vagaries. It needs a decisive role as all the current institutions have merely recommendatory roles.

> *Who will help put such an institution in place? The same people in power who are causing this?*

Hong Kong was once in a similar situation of rampant corruption. People took to the streets. The island was forced to set up an independent body with functional autonomy, headed by men and women of calibre, drawn from different disciplines. And it cleaned up the system.

The question is, who will help put such an institution in place? The same people in power who are causing this? No! It shall have to be the people of India, who need to be massively organised, educated, and informed to remove the enormous ignorance about vigilance systems in India and how ineffective they are.

Most of all, the people of India need to know that none of the existing systems are fully empowered and holistic. The state anti-corruption and vigilance bodies, the CVC, and the CAG can only recommend and the CBI is vulnerable to political control. The Lokpal proposed by the government is in the same category. It can only recommend but not take action and bureaucrats, who at times are the prime suspects, are not under its purview.

"We, the people" have taken the first step with eleven of us, including Baba Ramdev and Anna Hazare, coming together and lodging a formal complaint to the police for investigation into innumerable cases of corruption during the Commonwealth Games 2010 held in New Delhi. It is now to be seen how thoroughly and expeditiously the investigating agency delivers.

"We, the people" must stop being victims. We must demand return of the money looted from us and put the looters in jail, for life.

Jai Bharat!

6
Corruption in Police: Five Strong Measures to Stop it

I am on my way back from the 13 International Anti-Corruption Conference held in Athens, Greece, in which more than 130 countries participated. There were heads of governments (I heard the President of Greece explaining what all they were doing to make the government honest), senior United Nations officials, anti-corruption heads, government officials, volunteers, non-government organisations, and the media.

This is a biennial conference in which the international community comes together to deliberate measures to improve integrity in all walks of life, with a focus on public and private sector functioning.

I was a panellist speaker in a workshop on corruption in police as an invitee of the United Nations Development Programme. Along with me, four other speakers were also invited. I am sharing what I offered as my ideas on the subject.

I described corruption as criminal breach of trust, criminal misappropriation, criminal theft, cheating, inhuman greed, a sin, and a misuse of responsibility or authority. All these actions have an impact on the development and security of the nation in the short as well as the long run. Rise in crime and terror attacks are also a product of corrupt policing. Corruption is not only in financial terms, it is in intent, processes, methodology, use of resources, and the quality of service to weaker sections of society.

I offered five major reasons why corruption thrives in the police:

- First and foremost: When we have inept or transacting political masters. For them, politics is their personal business and reforms and service are just lip service.
- Second: When institutional checks on the use of power and discretion are weak. For instance, in the manner of appointments of critical leadership positions.
- Third: When decisions can remain obscure. One never gets to know whether the due processes were followed or due diligence done.
- Fourth: When civil society is weak, not organised, and afraid to challenge the powers that be.
- Fifth: When there is a fertile ground for exploitation due to a large mass of people who are poor and helpless.

Now to the five main areas of corruption that the police indulge in:

- First: Discretion in registration of crimes.
- Second: Dishonesty in the process of enquiry, arrest, investigation, and prosecution.
- Third: Being selective in inspections of organised crime dens, illegal activities, harbouring of wanted people, and so on.
- Fourth: Reduction in the seriousness of charges, or adding seriousness where none existed.
- Fifth: Misappropriation of official machinery or misuse of official resources—from a pencil to power.

We find that these five areas of corruption result in the following five consequences:

> *Combating corruption in law enforcement requires persistent action and pretended outrage.*

- First: The focus of police shifts more to protection of private interests rather than the protection of the society at large. The priority becomes looking after the VIPs all the time.
- Second: The police get distanced from the people and lose their trust.
- Third: The capacity of the police gets limited to mere firefighting. Lawlessness increases.
- Fourth: When the police persons become involved in criminal acts of corruption in various forms, they themselves spread antisocial behaviour.
- Fifth: The police leadership loses its control over the subordinates.

How do we reverse the situation?

Here are the five measures I proposed in the workshop for our country:

- First: India should consider the ratification and implementation of the UN convention against corruption.
- Second: An annual survey of the nation-wide and state-wide perception of the police service should be conducted. This should be government funded but carried out by a joint group of academics, NGOs and police persons. The results of the survey should be publicly debated for wider appreciation.
- Third: There is a dire need for a proactive, robust civil society. Concepts such as www.saferindia.com and

www.indiapolice.in need to become national movements to balance police discretion in registering crimes and subsequent processes.
- Fourth: Youth, starting from graduate students, should actively participate in policing as cadets to make them realise their responsibility in crime prevention and social defence.
- Fifth: There is an urgent need for a Good Police Index (GPI). This would measure the police system of each country holistically. The criteria can include use of information technology, training, welfare of the staff, updating of laws, media outreach, community and other relevant policies if made participatory, and the respect for judicial pronouncements.

Finally, I said, combating corruption in law enforcement requires persistent action and pretended outrage. It has to break the silence of many.

We need many more "bees" to "sting" the body politic.

Most of the key recommendations I made went into the resolution adopted at the end of the conference.

Regrettably, there was no one from our government in the conference, despite invitation, we were told. The rest of the world picked up these ideas.

7
Courage is the Need of the Hour

Two serious crimes have occurred in the past few days. First, the murder of a senior journalist who was reporting on crime and corruption and second, a minor girl found hanging near a police station with allegations of rape and murder by the girl's parents, while the police said it was a case of suicide. The post-mortem in the second case says it is a case of murder. Meanwhile, several policemen have already been suspended—to be reinstated soon, as public memory is short.

In the case of the journalist, the media fraternity came out together to protest, in big numbers, in Mumbai. They even heckled the Chief Minister and declared they had no faith in the Mumbai Police. They have said they would approach the Bombay High Court for redressal and have demanded a CBI probe in the case. They announced a fast as well as a march to the PM's office. They are obviously very concerned over the increased security threat to the media persons reporting on crime, corruption, and the underworld.

On the minor girl's case, the second post-mortem report says it is a case of murder, but not rape. This is exceedingly intriguing. Only time will tell whether truth will emerge, if at all. The allegations are against the very police who are investigating the case. Where do you get other personnel?

Both the cases are neither the first to happen nor will be the last. The Chief Minister assured the journalists that they will get adequate security cover. And called the top police officers to camp at the police station till the case is solved. I wondered if this is what will work. And the assurance of security cover for journalists will come from which police? The same existing numbers? These numbers are insufficient even for normal policing.

The point is, the kind of challenges which this country is facing currently need a very focused governance. It requires huge amount of effective coordination and trust. Both these seem to be deficient.

The journalists say that they do not trust the police force and therefore want the CBI to investigate. How many cases can the CBI investigate? They don't trust their own police. This is because the trust has been crumbling over the years and we never realised its consequences. The chickens have come home to roost now.

Police reforms are not looked as an issue at all. Policing needs a huge overhaul. But who will do it? Everything is politicised these days. But we have little choice. We have to deliver. And unless integrity becomes central to all our work, precious lives will continue to be lost, as in the above two cases.

Policing is a part of effective governance. It needs leadership of the highest order. What kind of policing will happen if the state chief ministers are involved in corruption? One Chief Minister (of Jharkhand) is in jail and another (of Karnataka) is under investigation by the state Lokayukta. The whole state in such a situation becomes rudderless. And leaderless! As is being asked these days, we are in a circus, but who is the ringmaster? Where is he or she?

Over the past many years, we have let matters adrift and are now paying the price. Every aspect of administration today needs a reform of surgical intensity. The common man is suffering. The media too, as in the Mumbai case.

In the last few press conferences, I have been asking the media as to which side some of them are. What do they want? Do they want effective governance or not? Then why are some vital issues not being followed up by them? Like when we started the demand for an effective anti-corruption authority, very important news was missed both by visual as well as print media till Anna Hazare sat on a fast. I recall many media persons came for press briefings without reading the draft bill even when it was on the website. Many wrote pieces on it which were contradicting what was already there.

What I am trying to say is that this country needs effective governance, which includes conscientious citizens too.

Those who are willing to work for the larger national interest are being singled out, only to be hurt, like Anna Hazare. In such a situation, only those with skin as thick as a rhinoceros will stay put. Those who are thin-skinned will withdraw.

The same media which is grieving over the Mumbai case must take stock. Being in police or media is also a mission. Of course, it ought to provide a decent livelihood. But the members of this mission have to continue to dare to seek change. Remain courageous. And take no sides. So that the corrupt cannot continue their activities with impunity.

What is needed today is the courage to speak out, courage to unite against wrongs, courage to question the wrongs, courage to take on the corrupt, and courage to ostracise and expose the anti-socials. As the latest Amul advertisement says *"Karo sahi daro nahi"*.

8
Tale of Two Bills: Draft and Graft

The government drafted Lokpal bill provides for two different and unequal responses to combat corruption in the country—one for "corporate " corruption and the other for bribes of the "common man ".

Several reports, studies, and opinion polls have explicitly highlighted the existence of widespread corruption, with victims across the board, and the maximum harassment suffered by those at the bottom of the pyramid.

The HT-C fore opinion poll of 2011 reveals that 59 percent of Delhi-ites paid bribes to several departments, with the Building department topping the list, followed by Sales tax, Income tax, Police, and Education department. Corruption manifested mostly in the form of bribes, 37 percent, and harassment, 42 percent.

Another recent survey conducted of expatriate business executives by the Political and Economic Risk Consultancy (PERC) found that Indian bureaucracy is the worst in Asia. "In India", the report says, "politicians frequently promise to reform and revitalise the Indian bureaucracy, but they have been ineffective mainly because the civil service is a power centre in its own right. Dealing with them can be the most frustrating experience for any Indian, let alone a foreign investor."

The report India Corruption Study: 2010, produced by Centre for Media Studies, after surveying 10,000 rural households in 11 states, gives corruption data for four key sectors impacting the poor—public distribution, school education, water supply, and hospital services. It has found that the quality of services is appallingly low and corruption is unacceptably high. Its overall finding is that 95 percent of the households who are asked to pay bribes end up paying them. This demonstrates that the grievance redressal system continues to be poor and there is a lack of accountability of public service providers, despite all official claims made to the contrary.

This is what Team Anna's draft Jan Lokpal bill addressed and provided for, comprehensively. Regrettably, the draft of the "government of the people" completely ignores this. This is why civil society has raised its voice against the government bill. Hopefully, this anomaly may see a correction by the Parliament and its Standing Committee.

The key difference in the approach provided in the government Lokpal bill (LPB) and the Jan Lokpal bill (JLPB) collectively drafted by Team Anna, is in the commitment made in the Citizen's Charter to be written for each department, proposed in both the draft bills.

The JLPB (Anna) lays down an accessible and empowered mechanism for an aggrieved citizen to approach the district level Lokpal officer for relief. The Lokpal officer could levy a penalty on the Head of the Department and compensate the citizen. This is the protection and empowerment which an ordinary citizen needs.

And if the Lokpal officer himself becomes corrupt, the aggrieved citizen can go to the Independent Complaint Authority at the district level. This mechanism is missing from the LPB (government). This is primarily because the government draft bill covers only Group A Services and no one below the rank of Joint Secretary is covered. Thus all essential services accessed by a common man, where central government officials are concerned, namely, railways, banks, post and telegraph, communications, civil supplies, and so on, have no remedy from the Lokpal bill of the government. And as regards the state services, the central government proposes to leave state matters to the state governments.

> **95 percent of the households who are asked to pay bribes end up paying them.**

Ironically, while there is nothing for a common man's grievances in the government draft bill, his activism is covered. All non-profit organisations, registered or not, funded by the government or not, but receiving any donation however small, shall come within the purview of the Lokpal. They are also expected to prepare a Citizen's Charter, specify to the citizens their commitments, be liable for the violations, and have a Public Grievances Redressal Officer.

The government, in its draft Lokpal bill, is proposing to cover only 65,000 class one officers, and excluding the four million central government employees. At the same time, it is bringing under the LPB (government) millions of small groups doing voluntary service or small events like the Ram Lila, Durga Puja, local fairs and carnivals, fund raisers for festivals or events. Organised groups like the Rotary, Lions, Jaycees, YMAs, Resident Welfare or Market Associations, Management Groups, small or big unions or mandals, sports groups, are all covered. No one is out of this.

How and for whose welfare this provision has been brought in, is a mystery. Perhaps to frighten the weak hearted. It will certainly limit activism, besides creating scope for harassment. An illustration of this is that if a Patwari does a corrupt act, the Lokpal will have no jurisdiction, but if a small cricket group in the same village does a financial wrong, they can be hauled up by the Lokpal.

Instead of the common man being empowered, facilitated, and provided an assured access to an effective anti-corruption system, he gets nothing from the government Lokpal bill. But if he is a social activist, and wants to do something for the society, and collects even a small donation, he can be answerable to queries from the Lokpal. As against this, Team Anna's Jan Lokpal bill had proposed bringing only those NGOs under the Lokpal which receive substantial government funds.

The government is continuing to promise the common man several schemes with huge public outlays, but without an effective anti-corruption mechanism. Without accountable and transparent systems in place, these public funds will continue to get siphoned off. The JLPB (Anna) had provided for a social audit, besides various other safeguards, which the official bill has excluded.

Under a differential, weak, anti-corruption system, bribe giving and bribe taking will continue to be a way of life. The message is, accept status quo and suffer. It is your destiny. Or do something about it.

9
Anna Fasts so We May Breathe Easy

The much awaited Lokpal bill is with the Standing Committee of the Parliament. Regrettably, it is nowhere in providing the remedies desperately needed to check the epidemic of corruption in the country. A historical moment in nation building is being lost.

The government's Lokpal bill is like prescribing a seriously ill patient a mild pill when it is a case of chronic disease requiring major surgery. Once treated, intensive care will be needed from caring and honest professionals, who have no conflict of interest and are committed to bring the country back to sound health, keep watch and intervene early to prevent any re-emergence.

Not a day passes when the country does not witness new casualties or even fatalities related to the disease of corruption. The medical bulletin comes up as "breaking news" through television channels, print media, or citizens armed with information collected from the exercise of Right to Information Act.

Heavy doses of medicine need to be prescribed and follow-up are announced as directional intervention—like the one announced by the Supreme Court to the Delhi Police in the "cash for vote" scam saying that since the court was monitoring the investigations, Delhi police must shed its inhibitions and get to the root of the matter and trace the source from where the bribe money came. What more needs to be said?

Had these kinds of matters been in the hands of an independent investigation agency like the Lokpal which Anna Hazare is agitating for, Tihar jail would have been full of high profile persons.

Let us examine what is the real cause for Anna Hazare's indefinite fast from August 16. What is his key demand? And who is it for?

Anna Hazare's fast is for the common man who is the victim of bribes every day. Every time the common man, with no political or social connections, needs a ration card, school admission for his child, birth or death certificate, water or electricity connection, wages for hours of labour, passport verification, report to police of land disputes or disputes with neighbours, and many such matters, he has to pay a bribe to lower level officials.

Can a small businessman do honest business without bribing officials at all levels? It begins with the peon outside the office and goes on to the official sitting inside. Where do such persons complain and who will listen to them?

So far the common man has reconciled to giving in. And in the government drafted Lokpal bill, there is no recognition of this widespread disease. Every survey shows that the problem of corruption is rampant at all levels. According to one recent report of India Corruption 2010, at the rural level, 95 percent of the persons who were asked bribes paid them.

Team Anna's Lokpal draft had strong remedies. It provided for a citizen's charter where government officials at all levels were bound to deliver the services within defined time frames. Non-delivery would be construed as corruption and the officer made to pay for the non-performance. Provision for public grievance redressal officers and Lokpal officers at the district level would have provided the relief needed.

The government bill sadly includes only 0.5 percent of the 1.2 crore government employees—the central government employees. No relief can be expected for the common man in this situation.

> *Not a day passes when the country does not witness new casualties or even fatalities related to the disease of corruption.*

Another important reason for the need for a Lokpal is that the Lokayuktas in the states have been weak in performance. Only Karnataka stands out due to the leadership provided and the inherent strength of the Act. The Lokayukta in Karnataka has the powers to investigate and even prosecute. It has its own Karnataka Lokayukta Police, which no other state Lokayukta has. And what it could deliver is for all to see. But for its investigations, the scale of illegal mining would never have been exposed and the Chief Minister of the state not lost his position.

Interestingly, some states, such as Goa, Chhattisgarh, Jammu and Kashmir, Orissa, Mizoram, Nagaland, and Sikkim do not have Lokayuktas. And in many states, like Maharashtra and UP, the Chief Minister is not covered by the Lokayukta. Most of the postings in these state bodies have become post-retirement rewards for the retired at the common man's cost.

These deficiencies need correction. But an opportunity is being lost due to lack of honest intentions. Removal of corruption which affects the common man does not seem to be the government's concern. It does not even recognise this as a problem. It wants to leave it to the common man to figure out what he wants to do.

As is evident, the poor have accepted corruption as their fate by giving, getting, or giving up and made peace with the parasites.

Join Anna Hazare on August 16 when he starts his indefinite fast for the common man. It is for the destiny of this country, our present and future.

10
Elections don't Solve all the Problems

What people want and what some of the elected representatives give are poles apart. "We, the people" have to find ways and means to bridge this growing gap. We cannot let the situation remain the way it is now. We have lost out in the past and continue to lose in the present. Do we want to hand over the country in this state to our children, or do we want to make a united effort to change it?

What do people of this country want? They simply want to be represented by persons of good character and administrative skills. They want representatives who will meet their needs, help them improve quality of life and living environment, provide solutions to prevailing social problems, and be one of them. They want to feel protected and enjoy a sense of overall well being. Basically, people want to see persons of character in positions of power—those who have a shared vision and are trustworthy.

Regrettably, in several cases, totally the opposite is happening. Many, though not all, law-makers have been law breakers. They abuse the law when it suits them. Actually, many make it to politics by breaking the law in a variety of ways like violent political agitations, riots, obstructing or assaulting public servants on duty, hurting or injuring opponents, defamations, corruption, and even crimes against women.

Due to the defective system, cases against them are either not registered, or poorly investigated, badly prosecuted, and remain pending for decades. Meanwhile, they grow in position public life. Where they know there is credible evidence against them, they deftly "manage" to either win over the witnesses or get decisions delayed. They even get some cases withdrawn, claiming them to be political vendetta.

Their background gets exposed in their affidavits filed before the electoral officers which come in public domain. Besides, the internet reveals a lot of information. The parties in power are known to use their political power quite often and the police head office obliges them with no-objection certificates, enabling their candidates to contest the elections, even in cases when their own police persons were injured.

This class of politicians keeps recycling. They stand for elections, get re-elected, and become the "representatives" of the people—even though they may have been elected by securing barely a small amount of votes due to the large numbers of non-voters.

Once elected, with whatever margin, the elected leaders now claim to be the "Voice of the people" of the constituency. But do we see them truly representing all and protecting everyone's interests? Do we see them holding regular consultations, through town hall meetings, where people could come and ask questions on any issue of concern to them? Do the elected representatives come back regularly to listen and consult with people in small groups, meetings, panchayats, or in the resident welfare associations meetings? Or do we only see them either inaugurating buildings or projects which have their names engraved on them, or attending wedding parties to get themselves photographed with the bride and the groom and give hefty cash presents, by which family remains forever indebted, and becomes a permanent vote bank?

At other places, we have stories of Robin Hoods. Recall the times when the dacoits looted one part of the country and shared their loot with the villagers sheltering them. The money from crime was shared. Poor were fed. Marriages were arranged. Many such kinds of persons were elected on caste and Robin Hood basis. Remember Phoolan Devi? This is how several law breakers, voted in by their beneficiaries bearing unstinted loyalty, along with many good and mature law makers, enter the Assemblies and the Parliament.

> *During Anna's anti-corruption movement, we were always asked who were we to ask for an effective law against corruption.*

During Anna's anti-corruption movement, we were always asked who were we to ask for an effective law against corruption. Who appointed us? Whose voice were we? When we said we were the voters, they said we were not all the voters. They, the elected ones, represented "all" but we were a "mere few". We were told that if we wished to get the Lokpal law, we should first get elected. Or else we were nobody to ask questions of the elected representatives.

Well, this is similar to going to a doctor and asking for the best medical care and being told to become a doctor yourself—or a teacher, or an administrator, or an engineer, depending on the need. If the only way to get the right law from lawmakers is to become a lawmaker ourselves, then the question that needs to be answered by them is, "What are you there for?"

It is time the elected representatives got the message. Otherwise, how will we change for the better? And leave a better country for tomorrow?

11
Electorates as Game Changers

With the way the last elections have gone, be it for the various state assemblies or the Delhi Municipal Corporation, the Indian voter is becoming sharper and more demanding. He is realising the value of his vote, even though elections happen only once in five years. He now knows the power behind numbers and that each vote counts.

The electorates have started seeing themselves as game changers. They punish and reward in their own way, as was evident in the elections in the five states and the Delhi municipal elections. The voter does not want to be taken for granted. The message is becoming loud and clear.

The Indian voter is also getting smarter. He does not reveal his mind easily anymore. He is learning to keep all power-brokers guessing. He wants the best specific deals, with a firm commitment that they will be honoured. Interestingly, he even seeks to know under what legal provisions he can hold promise-breakers legally accountable. At times a class of voters encash their votes for some goodies or freebies, but still use the confidentiality of casting the vote to do what they want.

Against this evolving scenario comprising millions of voters, is it not time for us, the electorate, to exercise our responsibilities post elections? To do this well we must be fully aware of what to expect from those we have voted to power and how we can go about ensuring or compelling them to deliver on their promises.

I am of the firm view that, first and foremost, we must never forget the assurances, promises, declarations, and written manifestos which the winning candidates made. Citizen groups must keep track of these to be able to evaluate and remind the elected candidates. Also, the citizen groups must reconnect with them as groups, associations, unions, representative bodies, with their changing needs which require urgent attention and action.

We must keep track of the progress being made. Ask for time-bound delivery and take the next commitment date before closing the meeting. The pressure to deliver must be kept alive. The elected representative must know he has no choice but to deliver, or else people would lose faith in his assurances and not forgive him for false commitments. There will be no support for him when he or his party returns for seeking votes in the next election.

Seeing the massive abuse of money, at no stage must we hand over cash or try and bribe our way through. Remember, no money comes easily. Every rupee has to be earned. All political donations must be made by cheque. The donor can ask for tax rebate as donations to political parties are tax exempt. Do not distribute cash and contaminate the system. A lot of our cash donations go into distribution of liquor. Of course, there are exceptions and all candidates are not guilty.

Every six months, active citizens must demand a town hall meeting with their elected representatives. In these town hall meetings, organised bodies must raise concerns regarding their areas, besides policy issues. They can ask for proposed investment plans for the area, the budgets, and so on. People must ask questions and also give their views on matters of concern to them. Let some senior person, who is known to be non-partisan, be chosen from among the people to conduct the meeting. And a group among them must keep the minutes. Let issues be raised with proper decorum.

> *Imagine what will happen if all constituencies evaluate and publish performance reports of their elected representatives.*

The town hall meeting must provide equal opportunity to all sections of society, including youth and schoolchildren if present, to ask questions. Most important of all, voters must ensure that the elected representative offers an account of what he did for his area or people in the previous months. Ideally, one such town hall meeting must be held once in six months.

Through these meetings, the representative will get to meet his constituents, get an update of the latest concerns if any, communicate any fresh challenges, and take a feedback. This means the representative gets to hear his electorate and update himself before he sits in the sessions of the elected body in which he represents the voters. In a way, he seeks a renewal of trust to raise issues which concern his constituents.

Once a year, just as there is a performance review of all public servants and other employees, so should it be of our public representatives. Parameters of the performance report can be decided, such as the quality of communication, speed of response, accessibility, perceived integrity, the quality of town hall meetings, their regularity, honouring of commitments, whether he takes people views in to consideration and adequately represents them, and so on.

Imagine what will happen if all constituencies evaluate and publish performance reports of their elected representatives. We may then succeed in arresting the decline in political performance.

Voting is our right but deepening democracy is our responsibility.

12
After Results, Remind the MLA of Promises

While on voter awareness campaigns, I share my anguish and concerns at what is evident during electioneering and the apprehensions thereafter.

In Punjab, Uttarakhand, and Manipur, voters have already cast their votes in the Assembly elections. Uttar Pradesh and Goa are to follow. Whether the electors voted with responsibility or not, only time will tell. By this I mean, did they vote under petty allurements or on sound understanding, with a determination that they shall hold the elected representatives accountable for their performance.

The VIPs come to us, the *aam aadmi*, with folded hands for our support during elections. They make lofty promises from the podiums: more reservations in jobs—even for rape victims, more schools—with or without teachers, more women's colleges, better health care (with fake medicines?), roads—without potholes, free power connections—even if there is no power during the day, industry—even if polluting, security—ensure policemen do not slap women, computers—without battery chargers, books and free cooking gas—God knows how, and even cows— hope not dry! Why do they do this? Because the *aam aadmi* is important, but only till the votes are cast.

But voters need to ask the right questions. Where is the money going to come from? How will resources be generated, borrowed, and spent? Who will repay the loans or will they be left as unpaid debts on completion of tenure? Further, are these promises being made for the first time? Were any similar promises made during the last elections? And fulfilled? To what extent and satisfaction level?

We, the voters, have been at the receiving end of humongous corruption and mal-governance. We are made to wait in long queues for getting our simplest work done, security cleared, and then perhaps told that the sahib is busy in meetings and we ought to have come after taking an appointment. Did they take appointment from us when they came asking for our votes?

Do the ministers and MLAs solve our grievances? Do we remind them of all the broken promises when they come knocking at our doors for votes?

Last year's experience reveals that as long as the *aam aadmi* has only a personal grievance, he may be considered manageable, for he can be referred to and directed or diverted. But as soon as he tries to represent the cause of a group, he may be in trouble. The person may be asked, "Who are you?" Or, "Who gave you the mandate for raising these issues?" Or, "You are not a representative of the people." The same person whom you voted for will tell you that it is his exclusive prerogative to represent your views, for he is the chosen one! He is elected by the people and has the mandate. "You" were merely a voter (not a vote bank) who voted for him.

Prior to elections every single voter mattered to him. And he came to even a humble hut to eat food and perhaps even spend the night there. But the roles got reversed as soon as the candidate was voted to power. He became the real VIP for the next five years and "We, the people" remained the *aam aadmi*. We were fake VIPs for few weeks prior to voting.

Our fate is sealed the moment we press the button on the EVM (electronic voting machine) to cast our vote. The question is whether the situation redeemable.

Yes it is. But how?

> *Do the ministers and MLAs solve our grievances? Do we remind them of all the broken promises when they come knocking at our doors for votes?*

Once the results are out let us, as citizen voters, insist and pursue the demand for a strong Lokpal and Lokayukta, which will ensure that the corrupt get exposed and the stolen money is returned to the national exchequer. This budget session in March, "We, the voters" must be prepared to come together. Look out for Anna Hazare's call on this. Most of the candidates, in their election campaign, have assured that if voted to power, they will support the demand. We must keep them on notice. Or else go as groups outside their houses and do some bhakti there to send them some purity.

The voters have to unite for clean politics and prepare for the 2014 general elections. The assembly elections were only a rehearsal.

13
Hear Yourself, Then will the Neta

Why did Anna Hazare succeed and the government concede? What brought the entire Indian Parliament to pass a unanimous resolution and accept the three main demands of Anna which concerned the common man the most? Most of all, were the indefinite fasts of April 5 at Jantar Mantar and August 16 at Ramlila ground avoidable, or inevitable?

Another question which is being asked is, what made Anna Hazare succeed in communicating the determination for getting the Jan Lokpal bill? Are there some key lessons to be drawn for "We, the people" and "We, the elected"?

As an insider, I saw the movement for the Jan Lokpal bill gain momentum and also hurtling towards a confrontation. I saw the response patterns of those in power, which drove it to extremes. There are two keys lessons for all of us.

Lessons One

Let me begin with "We, the people". We, the millions, have been, by and large, silent spectators so far. We were distressed, complaining, and brooding. We were accusing and even abusing. We were also distancing ourselves from the goings-on. We had shifted our focus to our own selves, our near and dear ones, our family, and those we were anxious about. The rest were outsiders.

> *Political and power wielding classes must not live under the illusion that masses can be misled or ignored all the time.*

What happened to those outside our inner circle was their destiny. We shunned political debates and reconciled with the politicians' histrionics and treachery. We used them and they used us, as the situation demanded. It was a transactional relationship. "I vote and financially support (underhand) you, and you do me a favour (also underhand) when I need."

It was thus a paid retainership. But on the face of it, it looked like one of polite acceptance. In reality it was one of the several "masks".

The situation made a fertile ground for headlines, exclusives, case studies, fiction writing, speaking engagements, regular columns, books, debates, seminars, workshops, policy groups, funding for such causes, travels far and wide, consultants, committee members, project writers, advisory groups, various forms of activist groups, cause formations, small movements, and many more.

These members, some very respectable, kept alive the parallel debate, dialogue, drawing room arguments, gossip, information, discontent, criticism, cynicism, and release of anger. All these had their own turfs and constituencies with very strong beliefs. At several places it was typical crab culture—"if not me, neither you".

The biggest beneficiaries were the scheming politicians, government officials, and those individuals or groups from other professions, including the self-appointed brokers. They were all secure in the oligarchy-user network, based on mutual misuse of national wealth, or the herd mentality living on the insecurity of an affiliated group.

This "people energy", creative or otherwise, never became "public synergy". It could not come together as a united force. The division suited many. Status quo was a habit. Many had reconciled to a give-and-take relationship. Hence the few individual honest voices got lost. The power centres, who were scared of large numbers, never felt threatened enough. People also never got a person who could unite them and whom they could trust. But there was a growing frustration all the time.

And the country lost over sixty years to deceit and the corrupt. Anna's movement exposed the pent-up anger in the have-nots. And while it knit them together, it exposed the divisiveness in the classes that had reconciled with the goings-on.

The lesson was—as long as "We, the people", across the various sections of the society, do not keep the interest of the country above ourselves, we, the have-not majority, will remain vulnerable to exploitation from the same people whom we entrust the responsibility to serve. Patriotism is the key value we need to ingrain in our children and ensure that they practice it. Only then shall we be able to ensure better future for our children.

And if we practice this, India shall never be short of Anna Hazares.

Lesson two

Political and power wielding classes must not live under the illusion that masses can be misled or ignored all the time. In the initial stages of Anna Hazare's movement, key persons in power were under the impression that demands being made could be dealt with by giving false assurances. But, as the movement gathered momentum, certain quarters threatened it by saying it could be crushed. The message was, "Just one hour notice is sufficient to clear Ramlila ground." In other words, to forcibly evict Anna Hazare and the thousands of people who had assembled at the ground in support of the demand for the Jan Lokpal, just one hour was needed.

The lesson to be drawn from this is that the elected representatives must be, and also made to be, on regular consultations with their constituents to understand their specific needs and aspirations. They should, truthfully and effectively, convey these to their "high commands" in the party.

Had both these lessons been learnt earlier, this country would have had no shortage of infrastructure, the North-East of our country would have been better connected, and our hard earned money would not have been siphoned off to foreign destinations.

14
It is a Trust Deficit

Politicians today, unfortunately, receive negligible public support for anything concerning them, despite being elected to represent the people.

The case in point is the ongoing wage hike for parliamentarians from ₹ 15,000 a month to ₹ 50,000, plus hefty allowances for travel, living and working conditions, attendance of sessions, and so on.

For many, politicians as a class have become a necessary evil. This is even when public representatives are apparently well greeted, garlanded, given gifts, and frequently invited by many for attending their functions. Most of the non-political families do not want any of their offspring to go into politics because they do not want a nuisance in their homes. Families already in the business of politics make a natural entry into this profession, which is termed as dynastic politics by many.

The political class of people, barring exceptions, has lost trust of the public. Often they do not mean what they say. They are seen as time-servers and they shift loyalties as situation demands. They are viewed as sycophants. Most of them are seen to be living way beyond their means and abusing public resources. Their children, too, act as bullies. This is an unfortunate reality. And certainly not what any democracy would want to live by.

The 24x7 television channels beaming scenes of rowdy acts of indiscipline by the elected members in the state assemblies and the union parliament makes the electorate feel helpless and wish there was a system of either "right to reject" or the "right to recall". Neither provision exists in the law books and perhaps never will. Since these amendments can only be brought about by legislative changes, would they, the politicians, do so?

> *We should have a performance appraisal, report card system, evolved as an evaluation system for all our elected political representatives.*

While writing this article, there was a news that a former chief minister of a north-eastern state was arrested for being involved in a ₹ 1,000 crore scam. He had been one of the youngest chief ministers of a state and had remained a chief minister for several years. I recall many of my colleagues in police working in that region, sharing in private conversations the known corrupt practices of this person. He has finally been booked through the intervention of the judiciary, based on a public interest petition.

There is yet another corrupt former Chief Minister of a naxal affected state in jail, who is attending the Parliament session while being on parole.

The Members of Parliament asking for a pay hike is being seriously objected, primarily for the reason that people feel that the politicians do not deserve it due to sheer lack of trust. It is believed that they already have enough money. It is public knowledge that more than half (300) of them are millionaires.

My view is that hike or no hike, we should have a performance appraisal, report card system, evolved as an evaluation system for all our elected political representatives. Their performance can be measured as they issue party manifestos, make public commitments, and get funds for development activities in their respective constituencies.

Is it not within the rights of the people who have elected their representatives, to know what their leaders have done for them with the funds and the commitments made? Areas of specific performance for assessment could well be many, primary ones being number of schools added since elected, number of dispensaries opened, mobilisation for community policing for enhanced security, jobs added, roads improved, quality of local governance, child care and gender issues, environment, and many more. The elected representatives need to provide proactive leadership, functioning as a catalyst for change through team building and representing people's needs.

One appropriate way would be that the new representative publishes what he inherited and declares what he would do, get done, ensure, promote, support, initiate, oversee, encourage, engage, expedite, offer, add, change, reform, and so on.

An independent team of performance auditors and non-political members of civil society could audit the public representative's performance annually and release it for public information. The performance appraisal, with measurable ratings showing good or poor performance, will lead to either appreciation or embarrassment. At least the voters would know the representative's performance by an objective evaluation which will enable rejection or acceptance for the future.

To be fair to the elected representatives, challenges or limitations faced at work and within the constituency could well be listed too. These could be non availability or scarce resources or unanticipated calamities which may have occurred.

What is to be evaluated is the visibility, integrity, commitment, and proactive initiatives shown by the people's representative and whether he lived up to his promises.

As of now there are no systems of appraisal. There are no objective assessments. People go to cast their vote grudgingly, with no idea whether the candidate they are voting for deserves their vote. And whether there are any options.

All this urgently needs to be overhauled if India has to be saved from increasing corruption and inefficiency in governance.

15
Government was Warned, but it Failed

The country witnessed an unprecedented upsurge against a common enemy in the form of rampant corruption, when Anna Hazare, also being called the "Gandhi of modern times", declared an indefinite fast to demand a joint drafting, by government and members of civil society, for an effective anti-corruption law called the Jan Lokpal bill.

The issue of corruption touched a raw nerve and all it needed was a "trusting spark" which could charge and unite the sufferers.

When Anna Hazare started the indefinite fast in Delhi on April 5, the people of India, barring a few sections, stood by him. There were men and women, young and old, urban and rural youth, within India and outside, and even schoolchildren saying, "I am Anna"—a sight not seen in India since independence or the Jayaprakash Narayan movement in the seventies.

Since then, one key question being posed by the detractors is, "Did Anna blackmail the system?"

Here is the inside story of how it all began.

Anna did not decide to sit on a fast overnight. He and his team in the group India against Corruption (IAC) offered to the government a working draft of the Jan Lokpal bill, made by leading luminaries of civil society,

Shanti Bhushan, Prashant Bhushan, Santosh Hegde, and RTI activist Arvind Kejriwal, through many consultations over several months. It was a counter to the weak Lokpal bill drafted by the government. Had the government drafted an effective bill, why would the people have to protest?

On the top of it, when Anna, despite persistent efforts, did not receive a satisfactory response from the government, he wrote the final letter to the Prime Minister indicating, once again, his resolve.

Here is Anna Hazare's letter, sent to the Prime Minister almost a month before he went on fast.

Dated: 8th March, 2011
Dr Manmohan Singh,
Prime Minister of India, New Delhi.

Sub: Our discussions regarding the Jan Lokpal Bill

Dear Dr Singh,
We thank you for the courtesies extended to the team of "India against Corruption (IAC)" when we met you on your invitation for discussion on the Jan Lokpal Bill.

At a time when the whole country is bleeding due to corruption, we are concerned that you expressed inability to act against corruption till 13th May due to ongoing Parliamentary session and forthcoming assembly elections. You suggested that a "symbolic" meeting of a sub-committee of Group of Ministers could be held after 25th March with the representatives of IAC. Rather than have this symbolic meeting, we feel that a genuine beginning could be made if the following steps were taken:

1. As written in my earlier letter to you, the government should immediately constitute a "Jan Lokpal Bill Committee (JLBC)" which should consist of five members of civil society (to be suggested by IAC) and an equal number of members from the government, to draft a Lokpal Bill on behalf of the Government. The committee should be headed by a civil society representative.
2. The JLBC should treat the Jan Lokpal Bill prepared by IAC as its working draft.
3. JLBC will submit its final report by 13th May 2011.
4. The report submitted by this committee should be treated as final and should not be subjected to scrutiny by yet another committee. Therefore, we request that such people from the government should be included, who either have direct power to make decisions or would be in direct contact with key decision makers.
5. The government should introduce the Jan Lokpal Bill as prepared above in the monsoon session of Parliament, with a view to get it passed through both Houses of Parliament by the end of this year. This was promised by you in the meeting.

I am continuing with my decision to start my indefinite fast from 5th April, unless the Government demonstrates its genuine intentions to act against corruption by implementing the above steps.

Yours sincerely
(Anna Hazare)

Were all these prior efforts not sufficient warnings? (You can also see all the previous letters which were sent on the website of IAC at www.indiagainstcorruption.org). Can the government or anyone now say they were blackmailed?

Anna sat on an indefinite fast because the government continued not to see the writing on the wall. It showed no urgency in tackling the raging corruption on a war footing.

The Jan Lokpal bill drafted by the IAC covers officials at all levels and assures prosecution from "mantri to santri". It includes bureaucrats and judges but insulates them from any extraneous pressures while remaining fully accountable following due processes of law. It provides for forfeiture of ill-gotten assets. None of these features are in the government's bill.

> *Anna sat on an indefinite fast because the government continued not to see the writing on the wall. It showed no urgency in tackling the raging corruption on a war footing.*

Anna's fast was preventable had the Parliament, while debating the scams, collectively demanded an effective law. But that did not happen. It is only then that civil society stepped in to fulfil its role.

Because Anna's personal sacrifice struck a chord with the suffering masses of India, can it be called public blackmail? Or is it conscientiousness of the highest order, reminding us of the kind which got us our freedom 63 years ago? This galvanized the Young India of today, for they got someone like Gandhiji to fight another war — war against widespread corruption. The only difference is, this time the war is against our own — those addicted to greed and deceit.

16
How should the Corrupt be Punished?

The answer to this question lies in how seriously one views white collar crimes of the dimensions of the 2G spectrum scam, Commonwealth games scam, plunder from State Budget (Jharkhand), or siphoning out of national wealth (Hassan Ali's case), with a total disregard to the faith and trust reposed by the people of the country in the elected representatives. Therefore, if this blatant plunder is viewed with the contempt it deserves, the criminal justice system should provide for day-to-day trial, preferably by special courts set up inside the jail premises. This will keep distractions at bay. And once convicted, the plundered money should stand confiscated to the State or returned to the victims to whom it legitimately belonged.

All this should send one firm message to everyone that white collar crime will not pay. Hence they can take the risk at their own peril.

The fact is, white collar criminals are comparatively more educated, craftier, and plan their crimes carefully — as they think — to cover tracks or trails. With money-power and influence at their command, most of the cheats tend to dodge justice and succeed in perpetuating injustice. This is why there is a general belief that white collar crime pays, because it is low risk with high rewards.

Corruption and financial frauds have created many undesirable role models for the youth. Fraudsters tend to buy positions, visibility, contacts, comfort, space, glitter, and upward mobility. Young, impressionable minds want to emulate them.

> *All this should send one firm message to everyone that white collar crime will not pay. Hence they can take the risk at their own peril.*

This perception must change, by making languishing in jail a certainty, as in the case of getting caught with drugs. This would be the most effective deterrence in the current scenario of corruption and frauds.

I also wish we could bring back jury trial, which will co-opt civil society in delivering faster justice. And in the event the fraudster is out of jail, let him be radio-tagged as in the US. It will ostracise such persons from civil society.

In the current scenario of rampant corruption and absence of effective and deterrent anti-corruption infrastructure at the different levels, we need to keep the fraudsters in jail and bring them out either white-washed, or leave them behind in the jail to learn how to come clean.

17
How to Stop the Fence from Eating the Grass

During the mass agitation for the Jan Lokpal bill at Delhi's Ramlila ground, I used to hold *"Anna Ki Pathshala"* for the thousands of people assembled there. This meant explaining to the people what we had assembled there for and why we must get the right kind of law now. Also, what benefits will accrue to each one of us if the country got an effective law to combat corruption.

I recall asking the people if they knew what telephone number to call if they wanted to report a case of bribe or corruption. Hardly anyone knew the answer.

No one was sure where they could go and to whom they could report, and whether corruption was even a crime like violent crimes or property crimes such as theft, extortion, breach of trust, or even cheating. The fact is that asking and giving a bribe is a crime under the law. They knew they could call the police at 100 for reporting any crime. But when I asked them why they would not dial the police to report the crime of corruption, they all laughed and said in unison, "Because the police itself is corrupt!"

Why has this situation come about, when the fence is eating the grass? The gatekeepers themselves are in need of watch, as Annaji says. This is the worst situation possible for a society to be in.

There are several reasons for this. But the primary one is policing. The country did not legislate itself out of the pre-independence systems of political and bureaucratically controlled police and did not reform it.

- When did we hear of any SHO or Inspector booking any top political leader, civil servant, senior officer, or corporate chief for corruption? This is when he books many common persons for crimes and violations of the law every day.

Do we mean to say none of the hundreds of known scams could have been detected or investigated and the guilty arrested and prosecuted successfully, in spite of having nearly 1.6 million policemen, in 35 States and Union Territories, including state crime branches, anti-corruption bureaus, special investigation units, economic offence wings, vigilance departments, intelligence units, and over 13,000 police stations?

Did none of the bureaucrats in the secretariat and police chiefs in the states know what was going on? If they knew, what did they do about it? And if they did not, why not? Has anyone been punished for non-performance or not reporting crimes of corruption?

Did none of the bureaucrats in the secretariat and police chiefs in the states know what was going on? If they knew, what did they do about it? And if they did not, why not? Has anyone been punished for non-performance or not reporting crimes of corruption?

And what was happening before the enactment of the Right to Information Act in 2005? Do we wish to say that there was no corruption happening then?

The truth is that our political and bureaucratic governance systems enslave the police systems by misuse of power to appoint, transfer, suspend, departmentally deal with, promote, and even reappoint post-retirement. They also keep substantial financial powers with them in the secretariat.

The reality is that to lodge an FIR against anyone mighty requires specific approval and support of the highest political authorities.

What, then, is the solution?

We must replace the Police Act of 1861 with one that meets the current demands of policing. A model police bill was drafted and is pending with the Central Government.

Supreme Court judgments may declare that the police are accountable to law, but between the law and the policemen, at all levels, there is this whole class of politically powerful people who block action and decide what should be done. This includes the police leadership which is subordinated by the politicians and bureaucrats, and further subordinates the rank-and-file.

In everything that I say, there are notable exceptions. But the fact of the matter is why, as a system, the Indian police is not independent. Individuals may be. But unless the system gets corrected, individuals can do little.

If the current anti-corruption movement has to take root along with the Jan Lokpal bill becoming a reality, hopefully by the winter session of Parliament, one thing needs to be done urgently. This is to free the police from political and bureaucratic control.

Let the police be overseen by a state police security commission or board, as recommended by the Supreme Court in its judgment of August 2006. This board can comprise the state home minister, chief secretary, home secretary, leader of the opposition, eminent civil society representatives, and the director general of police as the member secretary.

Maybe the Supreme Court could ensure the implementation of its own judgment in letter and spirit—a contempt petition for inaction is already pending before it.

Till this is done, police headquarters will remain mere onlookers to corruption. The Lokpal and Lokayuktas need to work in tandem with a politically insulated and rejuvenated police service, based on legal protection to whistleblowers, and reward schemes to credible information providers, as proposed in the proposed Jan Lokpal Bill.

If this happens, what a revolution we will see in our own life time!

18
Yes, Saying No is Still a Choice

As a member of Team Anna, I have been present in several voter awareness public meetings in Uttar Pradesh at Allahabad, Varanasi, Ayodhaya, Gonda, Basti, Fatehpur, Chandouli, and many other places.

My immediate feeling is that in our country the *aam aadmi* has gone through avoidable sufferings in the last sixty four years at the hands of politicians and bureaucrats, barring a few exceptions. I say so because it is the politicians and bureaucrats who govern and administer the country.

Every district has duly appointed government officials, who have come through competitive examinations, due selection process, and then passed out from training academies. After appointment they enjoy full security of jobs, completely unrelated to their performance. They are not accountable to the common man who pays for their salaries and expenses.

Similarly, every district has duly elected people's representatives at all levels—village, subdivision, urban, and rural. They are elected by the people and are supposed to be accountable to them. But in our delegated democracy, money and muscle power overwhelm the common man. Hence we suffer maladministration and poor governance.

Another reason is the existing nexus between the politicians and the bureaucrats—nil accountability and huge corruption. Each becomes richer and more secure, at the cost of the *aam aadmi*, his money, his vote!

> **Another reason is the existing nexus between the politicians and the bureaucrats—nil accountability and huge corruption.**

The elected representatives and the selected bureaucracy have let the people down completely. It would not be wrong to say that whatever we have achieved is despite them and not because of them. They have lived off the money meant for the poor and the illiterate. Their administration has been designed to keep the common man deprived and enslaved.

The common man is caught in a fight for day to day survival, which leaves him no time or energy for anything else, forget questioning the powers that be. He is constantly moving from one queue to another for kerosene, ration, water tanker, school admissions, hospital, medicines, fertiliser, and now MNREGA wages.

In all gatherings that I addressed, every time I appealed to the hundreds or thousands of people present to go out to vote, they asked, "To whom?" I said, "Clean candidates." They asked, "Which?" I said, "You find out." They said, "You help us identify." I said, "You ought to know." They said, "We don't." Or if they did, "None of them are worth it."

We were getting stumped all the time.

It was then that I was compelled to inform them of Rule 49-O as laid down under the Representation of

People's Act, by which the voter, if after seeing the ballot paper, feels that he does not want to vote for anyone listed, can go to the presiding officer and inform him. The presiding officer will record this in register 17 maintained for the purpose and put the indelible ink on the voter's finger as confirmation of his having cast the vote. This means, the vote is registered as a "no vote". The Election Commission will be, for the first time, making these numbers public, as informed by the Chief Election Commissioner.

In every rally I checked the public sentiment by asking how many voters, if given an option of "right to reject", would exercise it. It has been an overwhelming show of hands, to such an extent that it is clear that people may be going to vote more out of compulsion rather than choice. Or, as someone said on my Twitter page, "best of the worst" if there is no choice to reject.

In every public rally, the political *netas* descended from helicopters and announced freebies such as computers, jobs, free electricity, low cost loans, better medical services, and many more. At one such gathering, a voter sent me a note asking if non-fulfilment of promises was criminally culpable. I said yes, it was, under Sections 420 (cheating) and 406 (breach of trust) of the Indian Penal Code. I cautioned the voter that the police would register an FIR only under pressure from thousands signing the complaint. And if the police still did not take note, the matter could be taken to court, with all the evidence of these promises, such as news clips, manifestos and video recordings.

Are the VIPs from the helicopters listening? A new generations of voters is coming of age.

19
No Escape to the Corrupt

If you have lost something, even a small wallet from your pocket and you believe it has been stolen and you wish to report it, what do you do? I asked this question from the audience before me.

"Report to the police station, of course. Or call for a police control room van by dialling 100 and asking for help," they said, wondering why I was asking a question with such an obvious answer.

I said, "You are right. Now tell me, if you are asked for a bribe, small or big, where do you go to make a complaint, if you believe that taking or giving a bribe is a crime like any other? Are you aware of any contact number of a control room, or a place which you could go to, or call and ask for help, like the police control room van or the number 100?"

No one had any clue.

A few said, "Perhaps an anti-corruption department?"

"Sure, but where? Any one knows where it is?" I asked.

This is the question I have been posing repeatedly at speaking engagements on the anti-corruption movement set in motion by Anna Hazare, supported by many others such as Baba Ramdev, Sri Sri Ravi Shankar, Bishop of Delhi, as well as heads of other faiths.

The problem is that we have not addressed this issue of day-to-day corruption till now. There is no publicly known, advertised, accessible, assured system of anti-corruption available to the people. Due to this, most of us have become either bribe givers or bribe receivers.

We know we have to give bribes to get our work done, including even something as straightforward as filing a complaint at the police station. And everyone thinks taking "speed money" is his birthright, even to do the job for which he is paid for by the government. And unless that is paid, why should he work? He has no fear at all. No fear of being reported, no fear of being caught, for there is no instant reporting system. There is no mobile van with a number like 999 or 111 for complaints against corruption in which there is anti-corruption staff and civil volunteers to respond to any such complaint.

Imagine if we had this kind of a system? Anyone asking for bribe could be reported by making just one phone call. Every second Indian today has a mobile phone now-a-days, so the call can be made immediately.

The problem is that for the last sixty four years we, as a nation, are reeling under massive corruption. It has crossed all limits over the last few years. We became aware of it due to the media exposures, the public interest litigations filed by many missionary lawyers and citizens, and observations of the Supreme Court.

The amounts involved in corruption now are no more a few hundred, but are thousands and lakhs of crores. Recall the amounts involved in 2G spectrum, or Commonwealth Games scams. This is mainly due to fact that while we opened the floodgates for investments, we never created an effective and efficient legal and administrative watchdog to ensure that the benefits of growth go to all.

The existing structure of dealing and punishing corruption leaves many escape routes for the guilty such as delayed trials, winning over witnesses, non-recovery of cheated-corrupt money, small punishment, bail as a right, highly paid legal services against weak prosecution, weak kneed investigation by the (not independent) agencies, which enables return of the same tainted people back in power and position.

> *India is not poor. It has been kept poor by corruption.*

Due to these inadequacies, wealth has got concentrated in the hands of a few, creating an oligarchy of capitalism, leading to a nexus of the politician, bureaucrat, and the businessman, often called the *bandhgala-kurta* nexus. This vested interest today is directly affected by any change in the status quo. And many of these people are in very important positions.

Corruption has denied millions of our people more educational institutions, better health care, communications, infrastructure, social security schemes, and better prospects for all round prosperity. India is not poor. It has been kept poor by corruption.

The Anna Hazare-civil society drafted Jan Lokpal bill closes many of the escape routes. It insists on inclusion for prosecution of the corrupt, from *"mantri* to *santri"*. It includes bureaucrats and judiciary within its ambit, for investigation in the event of substantiated complaints. This means no one has immunity, if found corrupt.

We all need to stay abreast of these issues now as informed citizens, if we want to get rid of self-serving persons in powerful positions. We must remember we have voted them to power not to rule, but to serve the people. And they have to be kept on notice about this.

A few years from now, the same persons will return to the people whom they "ruled" to ask for votes. Before it is late again, ask for correction of all the wrongs, beginning with corruption. Don't let them escape again.

20
Spread the Movement Against Corruption in your own Way

Last year was a year of rude awakenings about some key realities as to why our country is the way it is. Here is an insider's view from Anna Hazare's crusade for an effective Lokpal bill.

Some questions kept coming up repeatedly.

Why are we suffering from serious shortages in our infrastructure? Why is there such a huge gap between the rich and the poor? Why is justice so illusive? Why has the common man lost faith in the administration? Why is there so little respect left towards politicians? Why are several of them perceived to be corrupt? Why do we not have effective systems, of which offenders in power are afraid? Why are our civil servants not accessible and visible? Why do we have deficient policing? Why is our farmer stressed? Why is there such a huge trust deficit between the people, the administration, and the elected representatives?

Let me share with you what became evident during this year-long campaign. And what we can we do as citizens.

Votes are like oxygen for politicians. They send candidates to elected bodies. As long as politicians know they have assured and secure vote banks based on caste, faith, sections of community, or sectional or cluster votes, they feel they can ignore even the justified demands of people who may not be part of their vote bank.

The next reality is that money power plays a vital role in securing votes. Many people attending election rallies are brought and even bought. Where does this money come from? Unaccounted donations and collections? Or patronage from positions of power? All meetings are also at the cost of public money for there is a huge infrastructure expense.

If one is in a position to give favours, considerable quid pro quo takes place under the table, as in the recent 2G spectrum scam. The money is needed in hundreds of elections to panchayats, municipal bodies, assemblies, and Parliament.

This money enables the infrastructure of elections—to generate volunteers, provide gifts or freebies like the ones distributed in the last Tamil Nadu elections, or liquor as is common in North India. This is the reason why corrupt politicians will not put in place effective legal systems which dry up the money supply, unless they actually see voters leaving them on this count. An independent CBI will spare no one. Stolen money could be recovered by it and punishments can be harsh. Why would the corrupt in elected positions vote for a system which will devour them?

What are, then, the solutions that "We, the people" have?

First and foremost is the voter awareness. We have to make people aware that they are the real masters in a democracy and the elected representatives are only their appointed "servers". It is the candidates who are coming to them with folded hands to seek their votes. Therefore, after their victory, the elected representatives are supposed to represent people's voice and address people's needs. Unless "We, the people" hold our elected representatives accountable, they will ignore the very people before whom they went with folded hands seeking votes.

This is exactly what happened in the mass movement for the Jan Lokpal bill. Constituency after constituency, survey after survey, clearly showed the support for a Jan Lokpal bill, but the elected representatives were not listening. They avoided coming to open debates. They knew what the people wanted. But they did not take a stand as they did not know the view of their party and its leadership. The fact is, people vote for their candidate, who happens to belong to a particular party. It's the candidate plus the party, and not the party minus the candidate.

> *Unless our millions of voters do not understand the value of their vote, this country will not get early answers to bankruptcy in governance.*

The message is that we must realise the consequences of being unaware or ill informed or being absent in voting and after the elections not seeking any accountability from those elected.

There is no legally binding way by which we can hold our elected representatives accountable before the next elections. So we have to collectively demand a way out.

One method, to begin with, is to ensure that the elected representatives conduct town hall or open meetings at fixed intervals. The dates of these meetings should be announced in advance, and voters should have the right to ask questions concerning the state of affairs of the constituency.

The key eye-opener has been that unless our millions of voters do not understand the value of their vote, this country will not get early answers to bankruptcy in governance. Therefore, when we know that responsible voting is the key to deepening democracy, why not initiate country-wide voter awareness campaigns to ensure that this time better people are elected?

Begin a movement in your way—small or big. Let youth take the lead and "vote for honesty" be the goal.

The movement against corruption has begun. You just to spread it in your own way.

21
The Enemy Within

In our country today, corruption has become a dangerous disease warranting a desperate remedy. Men and women, duty-bound to ensure the safety and integrity of the country, are seen to compromise it for a price, small or big. In such situations, we don't need enemies from outside, there are enough within the system.

Tehelka.com, a company which videotaped certain happenings inside offices, residences and public places, has exposed the scenarios of corruption in our country. There is a blurring of the line which separates the government from the ruling parties. The party members are the government and the government is the party. No doubt, the government is from the majority party, but once it is the government, it is not supposed to be for its own party only, it should be for the whole country.

The exposé has opened a can of worms. It shows how a large number of people in crucial and sensitive positions are willing to put their country on sale.

All this tends to confirm people's suspicions of the extent of corruption prevailing in our public services. It has lifted many masks of the individuals concerned—the masks of hypocrisy and pseudo-patriotism.

Public memory is considered short if the exposure is through the printed word, that is, newspapers and magazines. But the impact which the broadcasting of the visuals has had through the medium of television, and the visuals are likely to be repeated many times, will not be easily forgotten. The reach has been national and the impact huge. Today, it's the power of the picture.

It appears that the people who are taking bribes are still living in the old times with the method of acceptance while the givers are using new technologies.

The corrupt Indians, even when fully exposed, remain shameless. The words "sorry" and "pardon me" are not in their vocabulary.

Corruption is a crime of calculation and not passion. It is the constant calculation and the assessment of the chances of getting caught being low that encourages the corrupt individual. It is also linked with his position of monopoly. For whoever is unquestionable, the risk of being caught is at its lowest for him.

The effects of corruption are regressive in nature. Low-income households bear the largest burden of corruption. The prevalent corruption at the bottom level, like the corruption in the civic services, leaves the poor citizen deprived in many ways. It also has a paralysing effect on business, for it introduces imponderability in transactions and distorts public expenditure priority. Corruption is seriously detrimental to economic growth. Remember, corruption is also in proportion to the percentage of rule obedience in a society, and in the Indian scene, it is showing a rapid decline.

The situation has solutions, provided we are willing to act collectively. Some of the suggestions are the opposite of the three monkeys of Mahatma Gandhi who see, hear and speak no evil—now we have to keep our eyes, ears, and mouths open to see, hear, and report corruption.

Such "whistleblowing", that is, those who dare to report, would need to be protected under the law through a "Whistleblower Protection Act".

> *Corruption will not stop by mere disapproval, but through fanatical intolerance.*

Corruption will not stop by mere disapproval, but through fanatical intolerance. Hence people will have to be organised individually and collectively to express this intolerance.

In this process, perhaps some will have to pay the price, but then the price is being paid any way. The expression of this will power or intolerance has to be of both the people in power and those who vote them to power. The Parliament must bring about the pending electoral reforms and the Lokpal bill. All elected representatives and people in position of responsibility must declare their assets. The disproportionate wealth or assets should be liable to seizure. The law will empower such a legal recourse. The will and the weapon will need to be the two arms of the scale for balance and justice.

22
Three Orbits

A question being constantly asked is whether the reported criminal behaviour of individuals who are rich and powerful are cases of individual deviations or caused by the prevailing environment? My short answer is that these persons or individuals are a by-product of the culture of social climbing which overflows with hypocrisy and has got entrenched in our mindsets and is nurtured by us continuously.

The universe of our society can clearly be divided into three broad "orbits", as I would like to call them.

Orbit 1 comprises the "inner core". Rights of admission to this core are reserved for:
a) the filthy rich
b) patronage-based individuals
c) indulgers in wine or women
d) those with shared or common secrets
e) blackmailers
f) moneybags
g) blood relationships and those with a sense of insecurity

Those with any one of the traits makes them eligible for this orbit. Such people all flock together.

Orbit 2, the "middle core", comprises people who are sycophants, hypocrites, gift givers and receivers, repeat callers-on, name droppers, informers, flatterers, frequent diners, compromisers, and so on, and also friends via caste, creed, community, affiliations, sect, relationships, etc., as well as those with money to flaunt or expend. Any of these qualities suffice for membership to this orbit.

Orbit 3, is the "outer cover". It consists of individuals who live within their means, are principled, self-respecting, professionally competent, non-compromising, contented, spiritual, accessible, low in ambition, family oriented, bookish, simple, cynical at times, with few friends, who return home after work, who do not offer alcohol or lavish meals if and when they have a party or can afford one, and do not go around giving gifts or asking for favours. They seek no wrong help and give none. Such people are generally unacceptable for admission to positions requiring individuals of the kind Orbit 1 and Orbit 2 can provide.

Experience is repeatedly showing that quite a few of the high profile (socially considered) persons and positions usually gravitate to Orbit 1, many others to Orbit 2, and few to Orbit 3.

Experience also shows that, over time, transformation or transfer from Orbit 1 to Orbit 3, or vice versa, comes rather late in the day for many, unless, of course, there is a reformative experience or serious compulsion or necessity caused by a trauma.

Most of the incidents of individuals in the limelight in the past, present, or future will remain a "monopoly" of those belonging to Orbit 1 primarily, and Orbit 2 to a lesser extent.

If we are all disturbed collectively about the present situation, and want a change or correction, then the public perceptions of differentiating the worthy from the unworthy will have to change. Publicly rewarding and continuing to give public space and high visibility to people of dubious character, instead of ostracising them, is the biggest contaminator of vulnerable minds.

Personnel policies of appointments in government services also require to be regularly brain-stormed in a decentralised manner, before adoption and implementation. Regular reviews of performance would have to be integral to the system so that these policies continue to be corrected and improved.

Additionally, we require to re-educate ourselves to respect the law and be subservient to it *equally*. I emphasise the word "equally" because we are, in reality, unequal before the majesty of the law.

The law itself does not differentiate between parties or persons, but the processes of law, in their practice, cause the divisions. We have one set of rules and processes for one person and completely another one for the other. The interpretations change, based on strength and access to knowledge, intellect, resources, position, stature, clout, impact, social expectations, or anticipated fallouts.

The kind of apathy we show in dealing with economic offences, and social acceptance and even respect of economic offenders, is the most visible proof of this situation today. A small pick-pocket spends years in jail, while a crorepati who swindles the country of crores, walks free. The tragedy is that the tribe of crorepati swindlers is outnumbering the small pick-pockets, but we have no jails for them.

The ideal is needed but does not always happen. There is a huge case for sharing and surrendering of power and resources by all those individuals who are storing, hoarding, usurping, accumulating power and resources alike. I have my doubts if this can happen, except by a strong quirk of providence or the destiny of this country. But miracles do happen. We do have individuals who can perform the miracles, but they belong to Orbit 3.

> *We require to re-educate ourselves to respect the law and be subservient to it equally.*

Till that happens, Orbit 1 and Orbit 2 will continue to rule the roost and sabotage the systems from within. Orbit 3 persons or institutions, straying into sensitive positions, will continue to take the risks of doing their duty and serving the nation. And, of course, there shall always be enough for the print and visual media to stay in business and get the TRPs and asking the same questions again and again on the "Big Fights".

23
Wages of Fighting for a Cause

Policing for me always stood for the "power to prevent" and the "power to correct". The power to arrest is to be used for prevention and correction and at no stage is it to be to perpetuate injustice, for power play, or personal gain.

This remained the mission statement during my entire service. All my actions were dedicated to police and prison reforms and working for the marginalised, who are deprived of opportunities of the kind we received to grow and prosper.

It is this belief in the power of prevention that made me work as a social worker also during my service. I could use the goodwill I had for larger good and propel social reform. And it worked. I could ask for help for others—and get it.

Reforming and correcting people became an important part of my activities. I started my reform processes in 1980, with the rehabilitation of erstwhile bootleggers and got them out of their livelihood of selling illicit liquor during my very first district police assignment. From this, I moved on to running drug de-addiction centres in 1986, from police stations—something unheard of.

Now the challenge was not bootlegging, as the government had opened country liquor shops selling cheap, good quality liquor, but drug abuse. Drug abuse and crime were two sides of the same coin. Providing treatment proved the power of prevention. For the treated persons it made a lot of difference. Since the work had to go on, an NGO was born.

> *The work has multiplied now. It today reaches out to thousands every single day and makes a huge difference to their lives.*

From drug abuse treatment, my activities moved to education of children of ragpickers who were prone to joining burglary and pick-pocketing gangs. Their mothers sold drugs for livelihood and knew no other work. I set up vocational training centres for women and schools for children. The activities were managed through donations in money and in kind.

The work has multiplied now. It today reaches out to thousands every single day and makes a huge difference to their lives. Some of our former students are on the staff and earn honourable livelihoods.

I got another opportunity in 1994 to do even more, with the receipt of Ramon Magsaysay Award. Thus was born the India Vision Foundation. I did not name it "Kiran Bedi Foundation", for it was India that had given me everything.

As my first personal donation from the award money, I set up a bread-making factory inside Tihar Jail, called India Vision Bread Unit, to provide fresh bread daily to 10,000 inmates of the jail. This venture is today grossing crores of rupees annually. The income generated is being used for various welfare activities of prisoners.

Along with this, I institutionalised the playschool for

children who come inside the jail with their mothers. The foundation also trains women as crèche workers.

I generated funds for all these causes from several of my personal sources, including reward money received over the years, all speaking fees, all writing honorariums, all book royalties, promotional gains, savings from travel tickets including gallantry concessions, and donations from friends.

Travel for causes was based on invitations received, including invitations from corporate bodies and social organisations. A travel agency owned by a fellow trustee issued all the tickets, business or economy, and received and acknowledged all payments to the account. They duly maintained the accounting records. For worthy invitations, which could not offer any travel expense, the cost was met from the existing savings in the same travel account with the travel agency.

In none of the accounting or saving was there any personal financial gain for me. On the contrary, I stretched out to causes by investing my own personal self. But little did I realise that it would be misconstrued to the extent that my lifelong integrity will be placed in doubt by powerful vested interests out to victimise and teach me a lesson for being the voice with Anna Hazare against corruption.

Currently, I am collecting all the brickbats being thrown at me to build a Jan Lokpal bill. This bill will give us a legal system which will save the country from the corrupt, who are only getting richer by the day, depriving the common man of the essential infrastructure.

If we were not corrupt, NGOs would not have had to do what most of them are doing. There would have been many more schools, hospitals, dispensaries in each village and town, genuine medicines—not fake, more doctors and nurses in remote areas, the weak and the poor would not die for want of medical care, more roads which provided safety and not hazards as they currently do, more polytechnics, vocational schools, colleges, IITs, IIMs, and engineering and medical colleges for our millions of youth.

Most of all, audit at every stage would ensure that no hard-earned money is lost due to leakages. There will be adequate social security for the elderly and sons alone will not be the only source of security. Daughters too will be welcome and allowed to be born in the world's largest democracy.

24
Why are We the Land of Scams

When we think of crime, what instantly comes to mind are the violent ones such as bomb blasts, murders, gang rapes, violent robberies, kidnappings for ransom, assault, and so on. As a public we demand exemplary punishment such as life or death sentence for these.

But, as a society, we have not been demanding this kind of punishment for the crime of corruption, which is outright plunder of precious public resources, to the extent of sixteen billion dollars each year, as reported by Global Financial Integrity, a Washington-based research group.

While violent crimes cause social outcry, large scale corruption does not, even though it impacts millions. So we do not see the same social fervour in registration of an FIR, or arrest, or recovery, or prosecution and punishment for crimes of corruption.

Public memory being short, each new scam sends the earlier ones into oblivion. The cheat, whether an individual or a group or an entity, benefits enormously, while the victims continue to fight on, at a further financial and legal cost. Meanwhile, the cheated wealth changes many hands and territories to the extent that it becomes almost untraceable and non-recoverable. History is witness to this.

The fact is that we, as a nation, did not create effective infrastructure to punish corruption. The victim literally has no place to go to. If he goes to the police station, he is told it is a civil matter. If he goes to court, he gets into the traffic jam of cases. Meanwhile, the cheat continues to benefit from the swindled money. Subsequently, the perpetrator procures bail and lets the matter drag on for years. Some even disappear with all the proceeds. The larger message prevails—bigger the plunder, weaker the punishment system.

> *In reality, none of the executive agencies are independent enough to enquire or investigate corruption in high offices.*

Economic growth and free markets, with all their advantages, also gave rise to the crime of corruption in the government and private sector. Police stations are inadequately equipped to deal with even the day-to-day law and order problems. Crimes of Section 420 IPC (cheating) are the least likely to be registered at the police station level, or successfully prosecuted, for want of officers with investigation skills, non-separation of investigation duties from law-and-order work, and inadequate support from forensic labs to achieve exemplary convictions. The recovery of cheated money is almost out of the question as the system is least geared up for that.

The country needs a total overhaul, from top to bottom—from police station level to the central agencies, the criminal justice infrastructure (software and hardware)—to deal with the swindling and corruption.

Let us examine the existing infrastructure from the top. We have all heard of the CBI (Central Bureau of Investigation). This is one central agency which currently investigates many serious crimes, but was primarily constituted for white collar crimes. Regretfully, it has not been able to inculcate trust and faith, because of its history of blowing "hot and cold" according to the political weather. The CVC (Central Vigilance Commission) has also been in the news in the matter of its chief having a criminal case pending against him. Even otherwise, it is a recommendatory body and cannot enforce its directions. The same is the situation with state vigilance bodies. They are all under the same bosses and merely recommendatory. Due to this, the culprits, with the right connections at the right places, get away.

Lokayuktas constituted by the respective states to enquire into corruption at higher places are in no better situation. They are more of an expense. Whatever they investigate or enquire, is once again recommendatory. The Lokayuktas are headed by retired members of the judiciary, whose advice is ignored or their tenures cut short with change of governments. The Indian Parliament has had the Lokpal bill pending before it since 1967. It's still an unimplemented agenda.

In reality, none of the executive agencies are independent enough to enquire or investigate corruption in high offices. This is why corruption in India has flourished and made persons in discretionary positions greedier and almost unafraid of getting caught or recovery of plundered wealth from them,

In the last few years, the scale of corruption assumed such shameless and shocking proportions that India started to be called the Land of Scams. The Indian Parliament has not been functioning over the demand for a Joint Parliamentary Committee to enquire into the systems failure in spectrum allocation which led to a loss of over 1.7 lakh crores to the national exchequer, as estimated by the Comptroller and Auditor General of India.

The challenge before us Indians is to remain alert from now on and study carefully the kind of Lokpal bill the Parliament brings at the central level. We do not need one which is a non-starter, but need one which is independent, led by fair selection, fixed tenures, and transparent in its functioning. The prosecution should follow established norms of culpability, with time bound trials, recovery of ill-gotten wealth, and removal from positions of influence.

A draft model of the right kind of Lokpal bill has been posted on the website www.indiaagainstcorruption.org. Please join the national movement to secure our country's future.

25
Will We See a Change in our Lifetime?

I have been following the multi-crore stamp paper fraud case, also termed the Telgi scam, from the news reports on the internet, thousands of miles away from home. For me, as an Indian, the whole happening raises a very alarming concern. Here is a crime of extraordinary dimensions, which has directly starved the national treasury of thousands of crores of rupees in revenue. It has also cheated the innocent millions who bought the fraudulent papers, thinking them to be genuine.

The accused got the stamp paper printing machines and other similar sensitive equipment when they were auctioned, instead of being dismantled and cannibalised. They, then, received the vendor's licences for selling stamp paper. Many senior police officers are in jail, including the former Mumbai Police Commissioner.

What more evidence do we need of the total vulnerability of our law-enforcement machinery to the proverbial police–mafia–politician nexus? We are all obviously up for sale!

The credit of exposing this national crime, as I understand, ironically goes to a courageous in-house report and subsequent investigations made by police officers from the same flock. This report was picked up by the media, and then fearlessly presented to the Bombay High Court, through a public interest litigation (PIL) petition. But for this act, perhaps this national fraud would have gone on and on.

The police-mafia-politician nexus is seen everywhere.

The police-mafia-politician nexus is seen everywhere, such as it happened in this case, as I understand: The police taking the accused for holidays to seaside resorts at a price, booking the wrong persons, police officers driving imported cars without having the legal income to pay for them, depending more on informers and less on internal intelligence, and so on.

The politicians sworn to protect the country's security and integrity are, instead, putting these on sale. Elected members enjoy free hospitality at five-star hotels and the bills are picked up by persons of dubious credentials, murders of key witnesses and the main accused not being booked, and so on. No one looks at the disproportionate assets of the accused in custody. They blatantly display their ill-gotten wealth.

What about the onus on the landlord if his premises are used for criminal activities? What is the police responsibility where such blatant crimes go on, even before these are reported? Who ensures that the investigation is not dishonest and that the main accused are not let off without even being charge-sheeted? Who ensure that there is a character verification done before dubious persons become members and office bearers of political parties?

Who makes sure that reports submitted by enquiry officers are responded to by the seniors and supervisors in a time-bound manner in order to remain accountable, that cases are not claimed to be worked out and charge-sheeted or closed without booking the real culprits, that is, the kingpins? Who makes sure that case registration in the police station is not used as a cover-up for the people but as an initiation for the process of justice?

We will have to seek convincing solutions to these thorny, entrenched, illegitimate, and illegal systems that allow the "Telgis" to not only survive, but also flourish. And the media will have to persevere and make space for reporting such vital elements for our national security. Public memory may be short, but the media need not be short on it, too.

And thank God for these PILs of Anna Hazare and his team and the honourable judges. Let no one forget that follow-ups are essential to complete the surgery. Or else we will all continue to be affected by this cancer in one form or the other.

Will we see a change in our own lifetime?

If Indian democracy has to go beyond the casting and counting of votes, then the Indian citizens have to demand for ways and means to check corruption and the police-mafia-politician nexus that contributes to it.

26
Live in Resolution, Not Conflict

The country is yearning for a comprehensive and effective system to prevent and punish corruption at all levels.

The huge disconnect between the elected and the electorate is a stark reality. But as soon as it nears election time the same "seekers" return to beg for a fresh mandate, with folded hands, before the mass of civil society, who they think ought not to question them after having voted them in.

People have been helplessly witnessing their representatives "bulge" in corruption and yet get re-elected at their cost. There being no right to reject, they have been compelled to choose between the devil and the deep blue sea. There prevails a huge trust deficit.

But the voters are changing today. They are better informed, thanks to technology and media. They want to be engaged and heard.

When the people, under the leadership of Anna Hazare, agitated for an independent anti-corruption authority, it was after years of shameless exposure of national plunder, with disproportionate official response to arrest it. It laid bare the huge inadequacy of the existing enforcement machinery.

Under external and internal pressure, the government resurrected and dusted up a forty two year old "hibernating" Lokpal bill. Due to its own compulsions, it came up with a very weak version. It was then that the civil society stepped in and drafted a strong counter to create a comprehensive anti-corruption body to meet the current challenges.

The rest is history.

But the key issue is that even after scores of meetings between Anna Hazare along with his legal team, and the five the government ministers, two strongly divergent views have emerged. The government version is a hoax on the people of this country. It confuses and muddles the issues even further.

Here are the key differences which establish this belief.

* On selection panel: The civil society's bill proposed two elected politicians, four serving judges, and two independent constitutional authorities. The government's proposal is six elected politicians (five of them from the ruling establishment), two serving judges, and two officials. This is the first major difference—the "government in power" dominated panel, as against the balanced one proposed in the people's bill.

* The search committee: This body is proposed in the civil society's bill to ensure a country-wide search and co-option in a transparent manner of the best talent in the country. The civil society proposed a committee of ten members, five being retired senior judges, comptroller and auditor generals and chief election commissioners; and five members to be co-opted from the civil society. This would have enabled an important role for eminent citizens of

this country in dealing with corruption. The official version has no such specific provision. It is open to patronage.

> *The huge disconnect between the elected and the electorate is a stark reality.*

* On personal hearing: The third serious major difference in the official bill is the provision of "may" and "personal hearing" after inquiry or investigation, at all stages, for the accused. This will give an opportunity for litigations and delays. The government has proposed the following stages: enquiry, report to Lokpal, hearing of the accused, investigation, and one more hearing before the final charge sheet. Even in the indirect case of any person whose reputation is likely to be affected, similar opportunity must be given. In the civil society draft, after a preliminary enquiry the accused is made to undergo questioning and interrogation according to the law—not prior hearings to share his defence or self-incriminate. He produces his defence before the judicial courts under the laws in place.

* On bureaucracy: The other major difference between the two drafts is that the official bill keeps the bureaucracy below joint secretaries out of the purview of the Lokpal. This means the common man, who deals with these officers for all his needs of services, is left to fend for himself.

* On delays: The provision of citizen's charter in the official bill does not make any penal provision for delay in delivering of the service, while the civil society bill does. By this omission, the message being sent is that corruption is only corporate and

bribes are "small change" which the common man must learn to live with.

* On jurisdiction: Another matter of serious concern is that the Lokpal, as proposed by the government, is one more stand-alone body. It has neither been given the Central Vigilance Commission, nor has the anti-corruption Wing of the CBI been transferred to it, when it will be doing the same work as them. The Lokpal is specifically barred any jurisdiction of any matter pending enquiry or investigation. Hence all past acts of corruption, if under examination, are barred from the preview of the Lokpal.

If this kind of Lokpal comes about, it will be one more wasted spoke in the creaking wheel of law enforcement and will only add to the prevailing weaknesses. Instead of strengthening the anti-corruption machinery, it will further slow it down. Besides, who will adjudicate on which matter goes to whom? Are we pre-destined to live in conflict and not resolution, Mr Prime Minister or Mrs G?

27
Watch Out for Breach of Trust

I was visiting a city I am fully at home with. I have seen it from the time I was born. In those days, it was one of the healthiest cities one could live in. It was hospitable, well provided for, harmonious, and most of all, easy to commute in. One could bike around it any number of times all day long. We girls felt safe. There was a lot of joy all around.

Then came a time when all got lost—due to violence and destruction caused by bigots. Industrial production came to a grinding halt. Cultural creativity was snuffed out due to security threats. There was a flight of capital and people from the city. Everyone who was able to, left the city out of fear and hopelessness. People lost jobs and stayed at home for fear of getting attacked. Usually busy roads were deserted in the evenings. Suburbs where prosperous entrepreneurs lived were deserted. All the hardware on the roads disappeared, perhaps uprooted and looted. Migrant skilled workers fled to save their lives.

But all this was decades ago.

The city of my roots does not seem to have recovered even now, as many residents of the city have confirmed. The erstwhile vibrant industrial supremacy has not returned. The problems have multiplied, with mushrooming growth in population and all that results from it. Pavements and roads are encroached by vendors and shopkeepers for earning their livelihoods. It was distressing to see all this, which to my mind was purely the product of neglect over all these years. In other words, poor governance at ground level!

I drove over heavily dug-up main and arterial roads within the city, with road projects under construction almost at a standstill, with congested, unregulated traffic, except during selected VIP movements. The information doing the rounds was that on the main inter-city highway, there was one fatal accident daily due to serious road-engineering defects.

I learnt that hardly any three-wheel auto driver had proper documents, be it the registration certificate or the driving licence. And authorities could not prosecute them for their need for livelihood or political correctness.

The lanes in front of the houses were getting narrower by the day. The residents' main doors were opening directly into the lanes, when there should have been some space between the houses and the road. This was not about the old city, which can be congested, but the new and urban "planned" city. By-lanes, which earlier could take good sized cars, barely had space for two wheelers now.

There were colonies of widows whose husbands had died due to alcoholism or excessive drug abuse. The women and children left behind by the deceased were so poor that their first morsel of food came from a house, doubling up as a school during the day, of the resident volunteer.

I was informed that the municipality was out of funds for it could hardly tax anything for fear of losing votes. The result—almost no money to maintain essential services such as roads, street lights, schools, and payments for pensions, health care, and other social causes. All of this was impacting the quality of life in the city.

> *Realise it now. Vote for the one who commits to meet the needs of the city.*

I wondered if these were all insurmountable issues.

No, they are not—provided the concerned officials dismount from their high positions and be with the people. Drive over these pot-holed roads without the VIP sirens. Place coordination groups to monitor projects which have dug-up the roads. Not give away freebies and empty the government coffers, but let those who can pay, pay.

So what can the citizens do? Is there an option?

Yes, they have to use the power of their votes.

Realise it now. Vote for the one who commits to meet the needs of the city. Let the civil society of the city, along with the youth, come forward and draw up an agenda for the city. List out all that they want. And present this to the candidates and vote for those who commit to honour it. For this will make them accountable after the elections. This may become a service-contract between the voters and the elected representatives. Till now, there are only unread manifestos for which the elected representatives have never been held accountable.

This is also the time to consider each vote polled as a vote of trust for what has been assured by the candidate and his party. And breach of assurance may make them liable for action under section 406 of the Indian Penal Code (Breach of trust). This may be a new political action and can be implemented by the civil society using the Right to Information Act.

Whether this actually happens immediately or not is immaterial. The fact that this could one day be a powerful weapon to compel performance by the civil society will be the coming of age of the Indian democracy.

28
A Template for Leadership

Here is some telling feedback from a recent discussion that I was witness to among a group of senior officers: "If you go by the law book, then what are we here for?" asked a local leader from a new entrant in the police service, who was going strictly by the law. This young entrant was determined to do what his teachers had taught him in the training academy.

Another voice said, "Some of the local representatives think that taking up popular issues alone is their primary responsibility and not legislating. They forget that the laws being followed were legislated by them." One person said, "Until 1990, the moment a riot took place, politics withdrew. Now, some politicians actively search for a role in riots." Said another member, "The police force suffers from a schizophrenic syndrome. It has a split culture. For survival it depends on politicians and for accountability on law. We need a clear chain of command." One senior person said, "There is a lurking fear among some seniors that if a senior DGP commands, will anyone obey? If appointments are not in the hands of the police leadership, then who is accountable?"

Can such despondency brook any delay in finding solutions in current times? Much needs to be addressed from all possible directions. But, most urgently, there appears to be a compelling need to restore leadership to where it belongs and clarify accountability. Once accountability is restored to the appropriate location or position, it becomes the sole responsibility of that person to deliver the trust. The accountability is visible and fixed. Either he delivers or gets out. This, however, does not remove or even distance lines of wise counsel. They remain intact. We need not fear that, for it is equally imperative that electoral accountability stays in place. But the elected need to draw a line. Regrettably, it is this balance that is now lost.

Often, one hears debates on "Challenges in leadership for public servants". This is an amazing contradiction between "servant", "leadership", and "challenges"! A "servant" is expected to obey all orders. He can be, at best, a good housekeeper, one who can be a good organiser, have the skills to keep the house in good shape, cook and serve well, deal with visitors and guests, answer phone calls smartly, fix appointments, keep confidentiality, do safe-keeping, attend to the aged and the needy, take care of children, and even drive a car when there's a need. But how can he have leadership? Can he decide to renovate the house? Or repaint it differently? Or get new furniture? Or buy new gadgets? Or send the child to a different school? Or tell you what to wear? So when the role is only routine work, where is the leadership which is synonymous with challenges?

Only a free person can exercise leadership. Housekeepers are never free. They are expected to do as they are told. They can be dismissed whenever they show disobedience or indiscipline. They must wake up before the master does and sleep after the master has retired for the day. They have no right to any rest. They are subordinate to their masters in all ways.

However, the housekeeper is the ruler when the master is away. He can steal, entertain friends, slip away, abuse the place, sleep through, eat what he wants or can, disclose information, and get away unless caught. After this kind of exposition, should we continue to address officials in public service as public servants? "No", was the answer in a chorus at the meeting.

> *Stop calling officials in government service "public servants"; call them "public officials". Their responsibility is to provide efficient and responsive administration.*

Thus, the first step to be taken is to change the nomenclature—stop calling officials in government service "public servants"; call them "public officials". Their responsibility is to provide an efficient and responsive administration. They are selected, appointed, and trained as officials for civil service. Once they are neither referred to, nor viewed as "public servants", these same (or whoever chooses to belong to this group) so-called housekeepers will have to necessarily develop a whole new mindset of leadership. It is only then that they will look for challenges that are attached to the exercise of leadership.

Changing from public servants to public officials implies respecting authority without getting enslaved, taking initiatives, sharing credit, breaking the culture of control, encouraging growth, acquiring soft skills, empowering people, being trustworthy, communicating more, practicing team work, having integrity, and working with a missionary zeal.

The challenges that public officials will, and do, face is resistance from closed mindsets, vested interests, from within and without, including family and friends. But the biggest challenge will be the officer making choices. The choices he will exercise will be based on his own attitudes and beliefs, his own needs and compulsions.

The basic choice that will have to be made by the person will be—to be a public servant or a housekeeper, or the public official that people expect.

29
Visionary Leaders

I was invited to speak to a classroom full of senior managers of public sector companies on the subject of "Developing Visionary Team Leaders". The participants were undergoing a course on the subject of developing leadership. The subject was a very interesting one, as these days, all over the world and in our own country, we see the rise and fall of leaders. The media is so eloquent about the happenings that readers and viewers can clearly know why certain individuals failed and a few succeeded.

So I decided to raise a few pertinent questions to the class at the beginning of my talk, regarding their perception of the current leaders. How do they view them? How do they rate their performance as visionary leaders? For me, this was a way of self-learning. Now, it all depended on the answers they would give.

There were around 200 senior officers present, and, one by one, I wrote on the blackboard what each individual said, so that they could know what the others thought. Also, this would eliminate repetition. I wanted it written so that I could come back to it later, for a reason which you will get to know as you read on.

It became a very interesting inventory, and ought to make all those who are in leadership positions today, in any capacity, to question themselves, whether they deserve to be in those positions.

This was how the senior managers viewed the leadership of today:
- They do not have accountability
- They do not practise what they preach
- They use verbal and physical violence
- Absence of sincerity
- They shift responsibility
- They practise short-term goals
- They allow rampant corruption
- They are very selfish
- They live and indulge in falsehood
- They are hypocrites
- They are insensitive
- They lack dedication
- They glorify themselves
- They are bad role models
- They have false esteem
- They have a herd mentality
- They are ignorant on many issues of national interest
- They have vested interests
- They are indecisive
- Many are often immoral
- Many are criminals or offenders
- Many are unreliable
- They have hidden agendas and wear masks depicting public interest
- They are power-seekers
- They are cowards and are afraid of exposure
- They are merely opportunists
- They are manipulators
- They exploit people

- They are very superstitious
- They are very arrogant

The list was really long. Once all the managers had given this list, my question had been answered. This was how they saw others. I now asked them to audit themselves and see how many of these flaws they themselves suffered from. I told them, "While you see the shortcomings of others, others see yours."

> **Work is not only a duty, but a commitment and a form of gratitude for all that life gives to us.**

Hence, the message of the discussion was, "Whenever you see flaws in others, it ought to make you look at yourself, whether the same are in you too. And you might find one or more of these thirty deficiencies we all listed. Remember, we all expect the best of behaviour from others without reciprocating ourselves. This is the reason why you were asked this question and it was recorded on the blackboard for you to see and examine yourselves."

To be a visionary leader, I explained, we have to have a passion for work. Work should be considered a form of worship. Work is not only a duty, but a commitment and a form of gratitude for all that life gives to us. When work becomes worship, naturally there will be a vision based on honesty, right intentions, learning of skills, and regular updation of knowledge. Such a person would believe in the power of the team and will constantly share and give.

Hence, to be visionary leaders, we all have to be our own guards, our own policemen. Before we see flaws in others and pass judgement on them, it is our duty to look at our own selves. We are responsible for our conduct towards ourselves first, and then towards others. Only then can we claim to be constantly improving and training ourselves to be a visionary team leader.

And what a revolution in national character it would be if each one of us was to police ourselves before offering to police others, each one of us becomes a guide for ourselves before offering to guide others, and each one of us practises on ourselves what we proposes to preach to others.

This revolution can start at any time and from anywhere.

30
Women Against Corruption

Should we not move on from the run-of-the-mill celebrations of women's day, March 8, to "resolute " resolutions this year?

There can be week long deliberations, before and after March 8, on focused issues such women's status, female foeticide, falling gender ratio in favour of boys, few women in board rooms, 33 percent reservation in women's representation bill pending in Parliament, performance of women *panchas* in villages, women's security in general and crimes against women in particular through various seminars, conferences, workshops, rallies, pledges, plays, delegations, memorandums and so on.

Besides all these, there is a need for a concerted plan where women realise their collective strength by coming together on key issues and creating synergy. One of these could be social assertion by a relentless fight against corruption at every level, big or small, bureaucratic or political.

This is essential because corruption is currently the mother of all evils in our country and women are, in one form or the other, its prime victims. Corruption robs the common person of scarce resources and contaminates all services from top to bottom. Most of all, it distances public servants from their primary duties. It shifts their goals to usurpation of wealth, rather than serving the people.

There is a compelling need for women, as vote banks, to become "people power". They have to come to the centre stage for social transformation which benefits all and improves the administration of this country. It is in their hands to create a whole new generation of moral and ethical values for strengthening the socio-political governance of the nation.

Here are some resolves for women this year.

1. Governance awareness: Every woman, this year, must resolve to upgrade her awareness about administration and governance issues.

   This can be done by regularly listening to news, panel discussions, reading newspapers and magazines, watching more intelligent programmes on TV, attending lectures which make them more aware of the political, economic, legal, and national issues. Women must keep track of political trends, court averments, legal processes, and issues being agitated and discussed by political and social interest groups.

   Women in rural areas must understand the latest rural schemes being provided to them so that they can claim their rights and benefits. They must do this themselves and not depend on others. This will ensure they are not cheated of their rights. Formations of self help groups and forming their *mahila mandals* and own federations will empower them socially.

   If in urban setting, they must engage in urban governance in their respective wards. They must know who their elected representative is and get from him what is needed in their area—a functional school, an equipped dispensary, available sanitation staff, regular water and electricity supply, public transport, police post, vocational training centres, family and mediation counselling centres, and so on.

> *There is a need for a concerted plan where women realise their collective strength by coming together on key issues and creating synergy.*

All women must certainly know two laws, the Right to Information Act (for governance responsibility), and the Prevention of Domestic Violence Act (for larger prevention). Both are socially empowering. All that the women need to do is just to read the bare act, which means the simple version without the commentaries. This will help them to know the basic provisions of the Act and make them self reliant.

2. From governance to values: Women should resolve to ensure they refocus on the value systems of their children and lead by example.

   "Youngistan" or young India is a product of family upbringing and education provided at the school level. And most of the teachers at this level are women. What kind of upbringing and schooling will they give this year, so that the right seeds are sown?

3. This year women could also focus on realising their own potential. This is to embrace entrepreneurship.

   Those not employed, should make a special effort to learn vocational skills to be self-employed.

They can learn to do business and identify what opportunities are available for them and where. They should also acquire marketing and banking skills to do good business. Self Help Groups (SHG) are the way forward.

All women in this country are not in the same situation. Some have easy access to opportunities and some do not. The challenge for women is how well they use what is available to them.

The ones who have access to opportunities should use them optimally and move towards self-reliance. Those who do not have easy access need to create, search, or demand access. Women could form a network to help themselves.

There is no one answer for all. But a common feeling of determination among all to improve their position from what it is at present is important. And then, be of help to others. In whatever way they can, begin with their immediate surroundings, family and neighbourhood, village or group.

Women must take charge of their lives individually and collectively. National health and prosperity is dependent on the strength of this resolve and playing an equal role.

31
Traders must get Cracking against Corruption

I was recently invited to Chennai to attend a state-level conference of the confederation of more than 5,000 traders' associations from all over Tamil Nadu.

Traders representing medium and small scale businesses, including first time entrants, celebrate May 5 as Traders' Day, when they close shop to come together for issues which they wish to highlight before the people and the government.

This time their main concern, along with foreign direct investment (FDI), was the menace of corruption—the variety of ways traders are harassed by public officials for every little matter, and how they lose out on their business because of the delays or harassment caused. They wanted a way out.

The trading community had joined hands with the anti- corruption movement in the past. They had downed shutters to show solidarity with Anna Hazare's India Against Corruption (IAC) crusade. Many had observed a day-long fast too, with Anna, and extended full support to volunteers of IAC.

They were looking for ways to counter the harassment of growing corruption. After hearing several of the officer bearers and direct victims, I suggested a three-pronged strategy. The suggestions given to them are applicable to traders' associations elsewhere, too.

The first suggestion was to start a state-wide anti-corruption control room with a toll-free helpline number. Whenever an official came to a trader asking for a bribe, instead of giving in, the trader should dial the toll free number and lodge a report, giving full details of the demand, time, location, identity of the official, reason for the bribe being asked, persons present around him who were witness to the demand, and so on. He should keep a record of the complaint number given by the traders' anti-corruption control room.

The control room, on receiving the complaint, should enter it in the computer and give the caller a reference or complaint number. After this, the in-charge should forward this matter by email to the Chief Minister's office. I suggested CM's office because the complaint could be against any public officer of any department and this office would know best where to send the matter for appropriate action.

The traders' association should then file applications under the Right to Information Act at regular intervals to find out what actions have been taken by the government on the complaint. In this way some public officials may get repeatedly reported. This may act as a deterrent.

Today every person, even in a small business, has a mobile. He must use his mobile for reporting his complaint and save the message as evidence.

Of course, all complaints would need to be looked into to check false complaints, or harassment of honest officials doing a difficult job, where the trader concerned may be indulging in something illegal. But then, at least the matter is being reported and bribes not being given.

The honest officer, too, can guard against false complaints. This practice can cut both ways. Because currently the whole matter of corruption is loaded in favour of corrupt public officials. People have no place to make complaints against corruption, hence they give in and pay bribes to avoid harassment or to reduce delays.

> *People have no place to make complaints against corruption, hence they give in and pay bribes to avoid harassment or to reduce delays.*

My second suggestion was to join hands with the IAC, to become its volunteer, and never give a bribe. The IAC coordinators help in case of any harassment when taking up issues. Also, the IAC volunteers show solidarity by coming together and joining hands against corruption.

I enquired from the audience if they knew that Tamil Nadu was one of the ten states in India without a Lokayukta, which was a state body to independently investigate allegations of corruption against state government officials. Both the major political parties in Tamil Nadu—the DMK and the ruling AIADMK—have reportedly stated that there is no need for such an anti-corruption body.

The traders need to become a part of the common demand for Lokayukta. They need to demand a citizen's charter which makes delivery of government services such as licences, permissions, subsidies, or grants, if any, time bound.

My third suggestion was that the traders' association should run business schools in every district for teaching young traders how to understand business processes and procedures such as how to get easy bank loans, timely payment of interest, ensure quality of goods, hygiene and sanitation, maintenance of their own accounts, and so on. Currently, beginners borrow money at a high rate of interest and get indebted for life.

The senior members of the traders' confederation announced acceptance of all three suggestions in the press conference that followed.

What about other associations and trades? There is a dire need for all of them to take strong actions against the menace of corruption.

32
Time for a Million to March here Too

Every January 30, on Mahatma Gandhi's martyrdom day, at 11 a.m., all traffic used to stop. Sirens used to be sounded. We were supposed to observe two minutes of silence and standing still wherever we were.

This January 30, it was business as usual. No TV channel reminded of the day in the morning. Rajghat had its morning visitors to place flowers at the samadhi, but no sirens wailed anywhere; no traffic stopped; no devotional songs in the morning on radios; no discussions on the fate of freedom, independence, and those who need to be liberated. The elite remained glued to their CNN, watching the freedom struggle in Egypt. They forgot of our moment of truth some seventy years ago.

Our moral doom is near. As a civilisation, we are diseased, for we forget those who fought for our liberty. Perhaps genetically we have a slave gene which has remained suppressed and now seeks to rise.

"'Hey Ram' is a cry in pain, and nothing else. It is a cry of loss, not of hope. It is the ultimate truth", is what Gautam Kaul, former Director General Police, wrote on group mail of IPS officers.

To this, another senior officer wrote, "'Hey Ram' — this was not the cry of physical pain but anguish at intolerance, bigotry and enmity. Let us on this Martyrs' day pay homage to all those who sacrificed their 'today' for our 'tomorrow'! Let us live in peace and amity. Police as peacekeepers of the nation has the onerous responsibility of ensuring this. Jai Hind."

This is what I posted on the group mail: "While in classrooms or home, we used to stand up still on hearing this siren on Gandhiji's martyrdom day. This happens no more—the TV channels, the radio, and the home guards and civil defence in particular, who have the duty to maintain the sirens (the equipment is now a white elephant), could have sounded these. But who gives this direction? The political leadership? It cannot be the bureaucracy. But the political leadership is not leadership which leads. They are only members of a party!"

Currently we, in thousands, are raising a collective and visible voice against corruption, all over the country—including large numbers coming from all directions and sections of society to express our anguish against the "scam" culture. For the first time many of the armchair and onlooker kinds came out on a Sunday and joined the protest.

As Gandhiji said, "The future will be shaped by how we spend the present." This is what we are doing now. It's not a day late. But it's now or never.

You too can do it within your areas of responsibility and influence in your own way, 365 days a year. Success will make this country would grow richer by the day.

It's a tragedy of our times that we are being led by people who are too distant to an emotional and patriotic connect. However, they are not an isolated case.

Let us look at the way media reported the people's mass movement in Delhi and sixty other cities. The thousands of people who were a part of the marches against corruption, for the first time saw for themselves the manner in which the TV channels and the print media chooses to under-report, undermine, and understate selectively.

It has also been felt that the media, by doing so, lost an opportunity of redeeming itself after all the accusations of being partisan or sensational. If not for anything else, at least to show that there is no bar on any caste, gender, religion, status, or language to a common cause and a common fight. Because this mass movement did knit together common people of different faiths and professions—something not seen before, though often wished for regularly in debates and editorials. Now that it happened, it was not shared with the masses. What a loss indeed for the causes under regular debates!

> *This mass movement did knit together common people of different faiths and professions—something not seen before.*

How does one counter this? What holds back people power, especially when led by voices which are neutral, law abiding, and not vote-seeking?

I think this is the key challenge before all of us today. How do people get heard? And what will inspire and revive faith in the common man that coming together for right reasons is worth it and that unity is strength? We may have our allegiances, alliances, and dependencies, but we also have a future to care about.

Its time to unite against corruption, as it impacts us all. And media cannot shy away from depicting citizen activism. Media has to go beyond "screaming" to "streaming", from scams to solutions presented by ordinary and caring citizens from all over the country. I wonder if we now need a parallel citizen media to break monopolies and knit together India's millions against corruption the Egypt way—time for a million to march here too!

33
Second Freedom Struggle is On

The second war of Indian independence, this time from corruption, is a national movement today.

On April 5 Anna Hazare, the Mahatma Gandhi of modern times, will go on a fast unto death in Delhi to demand joint drafting for an effective Jan Lokpal bill to stem the monster of corruption in India. This is to reject the ineffective bill drafted by the Group of Ministers.

Corruption in India is an epidemic. It is widespread and occurs everywhere. Here are some shocking results of a survey conducted by C Fore across ten cities—Delhi, Mumbai, Bangalore, Kolkata, Chennai, Patna, Lucknow, Chandigarh, Bhopal, and Hyderabad.

The revelations of bribe-receiving-giving are mind-boggling. (a) One out of two admitted to having paid a bribe to get their child's birth certificate; (b) One out of three paid a bribe for school admissions; (c) Two out of three bribed the traffic police for getting out of traffic violations; (d) Two out of three procured their driving license by bribing their way; (e) One out of eight got a government job or posting by bribing the secretary or some official; (f) One out of five bribed a municipal authority to allow an illegal extension of his home; (g) One out of four bribed to allow an extension of their work places;

(h) Two out of three bribed a tax official to evade sales tax; (i) One out of four paid bribes to continue flouting pollution norms.

Bribes that big corporations give, according to industry sources, are: (a) Land use change: five percent of land revenue value; (b) Pollution clearance (one time): ₹ one crore if it's a polluting industry; (c) Excise officials: ten percent of evasion; (d) Electricity officials: thirty percent of the theft; (e) Tax officials: ten percent of income tax refund; (f) National highways: ₹ fifty lakh per km; (g) Police: ₹ 25,000 per month; (h) Factory inspectors: ₹ 5,000 per month; (i) Boiler inspectors: ₹ 5,000 per month; and (j) Railway wagon: five per cent of the value of the goods.

This level of corruption is getting worse day-by-day. The bribe-receiver grows richer while the bribe-giver either "survives" or "thrives", depending on the situation. This form of corruption has serious ramifications because all violations have a price that we pay individually or collectively, directly or indirectly, as a society.

The bribe-giver contributes to uneven distribution of resources, fouls the merit system, pollutes the environment, increases human hazards, and spreads discontent and mistrust, which weaken the foundation of the country by producing corruption-tolerant generations. This, as the survey reveals, is what has happened to India today. The bribe-giver is under duress to give for personal or business compulsions, or is greedy to acquire more wealth and influence. On both counts he is an abettor and culpable under the Indian legal system.

UK has recently passed the Bribery Act 2010, which defines and clarifies offences of general bribery. It says, "If a person offers, promises or gives a financial or other advantage to another person and that person intends the advantage to induce a person to perform improperly a relevant function or activity, or to reward a person for the improper performance of such a function or activity, shall be punishable, on summary conviction with 12 months and on indictment up to 10 years. The functions and activities which fall within this scope are ... any function of a public nature; any activity connected with a business performed in the course of a person's employment, performed by or on behalf of a body of persons (whether corporate or unincorporated) even outside the United Kingdom ... "

> *No crime of corruption takes place without the nexus of money, position, and power. So both the bribe-receiver and the bribe-giver have to be punished.*

The Jan Lokpal bill drafted by the India Against Corruption (IAC) movement and offered to the Government of India, has provided for a similar clause: "Any person who obtains any benefit from the government by violating any laws or rules that person along with public servants who directly or indirectly helped that person to obtain those benefits shall be deemed to have indulged in corruption ... "

No crime of corruption takes place without the nexus of money, position, and power. So both the bribe-receiver and the bribe-giver have to be punished for distorting the system—more so when it is for greed and national plunder.

The Jan Lokpal bill, if drafted jointly, will ensure an effective law (see the one posted, and join the movement on www.indiaagainstcorruption.org) to win the second war of independence.

Anna is the Mahatma and all of us are freedom fighters. The Jan Lokpal bill assures that—to be masters of our destiny and not mere voters of the corrupt. This will be a victory for our future.

34

Lambs No More, Silent No More

Several questions on corruption are being repeatedly asked in many public forums. I thought of sharing a few of them as they were posed.

1. Why have Indians been suffering corruption all these past sixty years?
A. Because they were indifferent and, by and large, afraid and helpless, because anyone who raised the voice against the establishment ran severe risks of being harmed.
2. Did they not know who was indulging in what?
A. Yes they knew, but no one united them to give them a voice. They were kept divided by caste, creed, community, and more.
3. Was it not making news?
A. Yes, but not enough to anger and galvanise the nation. Prior to 24x7 television news, newspapers were read, radio was heard, but it did not create as much unrest as it does today.
4. Was media not writing or projecting the issues?
A. Yes, but that was not creating enough united pressure.

5. Did people know what they could do?
A. There was no faith in the law enforcement agencies which themselves needed to be under watch as they were susceptible to extraneous influences. Where do you go and who will listen? The systems of anti-corruption were either non-existent or only in the name. There was actually no place to go. Pay up or go home.
6. And what was our enforcement system, which was responsible for bringing to book white-collar crimes?
A. It was a politically controlled law enforcement system.

Look at the way the premier investigating agency, the Central Bureau of Investigation, is functioning. It has to take approvals from the same government whose officials it is supposed to investigate. There is a clear conflict of interest. It cannot appoint lawyers or experts of its choice. It does not have a free hand in its budget. It is susceptible to vagaries of personnel deputed from other departments. Post-retirement jobs are a big carrot dangling in front of them.

The fact of the matter is that a normal Indian below the poverty line, comprising about one third of 1.2 billion people, is struggling with his day-to-day existence. He needs help for everything—from getting his rations, to water, electricity, ration card, a roof on his head, a school for his children, selling his wares, bank loans, and search for employment for his grown-up children. There is nothing sure for him. In the event of ill health, he is likely to lose his meagre savings or go into debt.

For half of the population, it is the family and their support systems, barring exceptions. The challenge for them is how to improve from the level achieved by their parents. For them it about sustaining the basic essentials of life — a house, transport, friends, entertainment, spending on marriages, security, relationships, job skills, associations, social networks, and capacity to get their work done by hook or by crook. They are the first and the second rung of bribe takers and collectors. They are the inspectorate, the "file initiators", and "safe keepers", as also the first providers. Their primary motivation is self, family, caste, acquisition, and facilitation for seniors.

> *Look at the way the premier investigating agency, the Central Bureau of Investigation, is functioning. It has to take approvals from the same government whose officials it is supposed to investigate. There is a clear conflict of interest.*

The top one percent rich in the country have a nexus, barring honourable exceptions, of powerful givers and rich receivers of national wealth. Both sections get richer and more influential by the day, while making the field narrower for new, young entrants.

Why has this happened? It is because other than voting once in five years we do not have systems of effective checks-and-control and measures to assess the persons we elect. Whatever issues are raised, they are through the political parties, led by "high commands" setting the agenda. When civil society raised the voice against corruption, it was termed as "tyranny of the unelected"!

Civil society, under the leadership of social activist and reformer Anna Hazare, has knit the country together, demanding an accountable, independent, investigating agency, which the country does not have till now. This is the real reason behind the widespread disease of corruption and the mass movement to address it. People today are better informed by print and visual media, and armed with the Right to Information Act.

As a consequence of the "tyranny of the unelected", the Indian Parliament may legislate a Lokpal (Ombudsman) bill and also as a consequence of signing the UN Convention against Corruption. In the event of failure to pass the bill, December 27 is the date set for revival of mass movement by Anna Hazare.

The party in power can do what it wants, provided it has the political will. If it can pass a cabinet resolution for foreign direct investment in retail while the Parliament is in session, it can bring in whatever bills it wants or even call for a special session.

According to reliable sources, a majority of the politicians do not want a strong Lokpal, for fear of loss of power, money, and protection against certain acts from which they have been escaping in the past.

"We, the people" are back on the streets. Do you want to stand up and be counted?

35
The Way Ahead

A tweet I received as I was writing this article was very apt. It said, "*Our patriotic leaders gave us independence. Today we have ruined our independence with corruption at all levels. Our next generation will suffer our mistakes. Think. Leave a better society for your next generation. Happy Independence Day.*"

This is exactly the reason why the country saw massive agitations against large scale corruption. This corruption may have been hidden during the last several decades, with the criminal justice system deliberately kept ineffective. By this I mean a politically managed Central Bureau of Investigation (CBI) and courts clogged with huge number of pending cases, causing delayed trials, due to which there is not enough fear amongst those breaking the law.

Anti-corruption movements were initiated for an effective Lokpal bill to remedy these ills by Anna Hazare and for return of black money, stashed in overseas tax havens, by Baba Ramdevji.

But what was the first trigger for these civil society movements?

It was the massive corruption exposed in organisation of the Commonwealth Games in 2010. The media produced evidence of excessive costs, huge over-run of budgets, favouritism in contracts, shabby quality of infrastructure created, and so on.

Despite this, matters were ignored for a long time. The same was the case with the exposure of 2G spectrum scam. We all know this resulted in lakhs of crores of rupees of loss to the central exchequer, as reported by the Comptroller and Auditor General of India (CAG). It took a long time for the investigating agencies to put their act together and perform their basic duty.

Another scam was of Adarsh Society, where housing meant for war widows was allotted to persons with political connections. In this case too, the same hesitation was seen in nabbing the main culprits.

The more the activists researched, the more cases of corruption got unearthed. Once again, we saw the observations and directions of Apex Courts, CAG, etc., about serious financial irregularities and other acts amounting to corruption, against fifteen cabinet ministers going un-investigated. It was this which became the trigger for more agitations.

We all saw the just concluded *anshan* of Baba Ramdevji at the Ramlila ground at Delhi, for return of black money from tax havens, and prior to that of Anna Hazare at Jantar Mantar for an independent investigation of allegations against cabinet ministers. Both drew unprecedented support, not seen since Jayaprakash Narayan's movement in the post emergency days of 1975.

Now that these agitations against corruption are over, what happens to the collective voice against corruption raised all across, within India and overseas? We need to grasp the key challenges these crusades against corruption have thrown.

The most important challenge is for the *aam aadmi*—the people who are affected by it all.

All registered voters, individually and as a group, must learn to value their vote. A large number of them need to understand that a vote is "not for sale but for the right to be served". It is a sacred "button" power in their hands to demand good governance for their betterment and that of the society, from those who are coming with folded hands to their door step, promising them better quality of life.

> *...need to understand that a vote is "not for sale but for the right to be served". It is a sacred "button" power in their hands to demand good governance for their betterment...*

Elections are the time to assess—did the elected representative deliver promises made when seeking votes? Has the quality of life improved? To what extent has it changed since the person came to ask for votes the last time?

Elections are the time to evaluate—what result did the vote they cast the last time bring—larger benefit or loss? Did it add to the values system in society or did it weaken it? Did the person whom you voted for serve the area? Or did he only serve himself? Was he available to hear the people? Did he have a fixed time to hear grievances? Did he consult people before going for corporation, assembly or parliament sessions and did he ever come and give a feedback, by prior intimation? Did he inform his constituency how he spent the funds for development which were allotted to him? Did you, as voters, demand his accountability?

So the future is all about our existing voters and how responsible they can become. They should not think that their vote is a mere button which is to be pressed as a ritual once in five years. Their vote is something which can trigger change for the better, for the voter and for the country.

The non-registered but eligible voters are also important. It is imperative that every person above the age of eighteen registers as a voter in order to be able to exercise the social and citizen's responsibility. The announcements for registering new voters are made with sparse publicity budgets, more as a formality rather than as a serious campaign and information is scanty. Therefore, eligible voter need to take the initiative to register themselves and become aware of what is going on. Only then will the voting percentage cross ninety percent as against the current average of fifty percent or so.

Our democracy is sixty six years old today. This is the age of maturity. Every voter must realise that he is the brick in the foundation of democracy. If he wants the country to be strong, he has place the brick right.

Jai Hind!